Paris

for kids

Paris
for kids

CHÊNE

Contents

Chapter 1
Playing and burning off energy

Ready, steady, go!

Top 10 playgrounds in Paris

Naturally, you'd love to think of your little darlings as more than just potential nuisances who will disturb your tranquillity with their noise and silliness, and their constant and loud complaining of 'I'm bored.' Luckily, the French capital abounds with pockets of enjoyment especially designed for your young kids. Not only are they places to delight and entertain them, but you can also join in the fun with these activities for children.

1 TERRAIN D'AVENTURES, AN ADVENTURE IN THE HEART OF PARIS

The first stage of the major overhaul of the Les Halles precinct, this 2,500-square-metre adventure playground will fascinate children aged from 7–11. It's enough to make parents envious of their kids. This space is filled with towering climbing frames, cascades and waterfalls, canyons where they can play hide-and-seek, giant climbing walls, a 20-metre-long spiral slide and monumental sculptures to excite the imagination.

Jardin Nelson-Mandela, 1ᵉʳ. Open Tues–Sun 10am–7pm. Free admission.

2 A SUMMER PLAYGROUND THAT TAKES OVER THE SQUARE

During summer, a poppy-red terrace is set up in the square at Place de la République, recently redesigned to provide a living space for the residents of the third, tenth and eleventh arrondissements. Parents and children take their seats to take advantage of an extraordinary toy and game library. Board games; games involving skill, water, building; giant games; and many forms of outdoor entertainment are organized by the Île-de-France Toy Library Association (ALIF).

Place de la République, 3ᵉ-10ᵉ-11ᵉ.
Open June–end Sept, Tues–Sun 11am–8pm.
Free toy and game hire
lalif.org

3 A GARDEN SUSPENDED ABOVE PARIS

Forget the soft synthetic surfacing and moulded plastic. After the reign of health-and-safety culture, here is a return to risk-taking. A tree-house, giant slides, climbing frames, rough terrain, concrete, grass and woods at **Parc de Belleville**. Perfect for recreating the *War of the Buttons*. It's well worth making the journey here, even if only to enjoy the panoramic view from the Rue Piat entrance to the garden.

Cnr Rue des Envierges and Rue Piat, 20ᵉ.
Free admission.

9

4 PARK WITH PLENTY OF MILEAGE

Built on the site of the former Citroën factory, this futuristic park overlooking the Seine is anything but ordinary. Sandboxes, flying foxes, water jets… and a tethered hot-air balloon that takes you 150 metres into the air.

Parc André-Citroën

2, Rue Cauchy, 15ᵉ. Free admission.

Air de Paris hot-air balloon, €10–12 for adults, free for Paris residents under 12.

5 THE BIGGER, THE CRAZIER

The facilities at Parc de la Villette, the largest park in Paris, are absolutely insane: from the flying fox to the long inflated trampolines, by way of the dragon slide.

You can also have a picnic on the grass, walk through themed gardens, listen to percussion music and ride the roundabout. Be warned; the hook-a-duck game is addictive!

211, Avenue Jean-Jaurès, 19ᵉ.

Free admission to the playground.

6 A PARK TO RIVAL DISNEYLAND AND PARC ASTÉRIX

With heaps of activities and play areas, the **Jardin d'Acclimatation** is the third most-visited theme park in France. Start with the play areas (free), with their paddling pool, trampoline and distorting mirrors, then head for the farm, zoo, pony club, vegetable garden and puppet theatre, among the many attractions.

Bois de Boulogne, 16ᵉ.

Admission to the garden €3, free for children under 7. Attractions and rides €2.90 a ticket.

7 A PARK FILLED WITH COLOUR

Parc Floral is a magnificent place where the fragrance of flowers fills the air, and where you can have a picnic under the shade of the trees and let your children burn off their energy in one of its playgrounds.

Esplanade du Château de Vincennes,

Route de la Pyramide, Bois de Vincennes, 12ᵉ.

Free admission, except days with programmed entertainment: €5, half-price € 2.50, free for children under 7.

8 EXPLORING FAUNA AND FLORA

As its name indicates, the **Jardin des Plantes** is dedicated to botany: dozens of varieties of roses bloom to the delight of visitors, the iris bed draws great admiration, and tropical greenhouses line the central paths. The zoo is also worth a visit. In the style of early twentieth-century Paris, featuring narrow paths that wind between aviaries and pavilions, it has a quirky charm and is home to magnificent specimens of dromedaries, ostriches, crocodiles and various antelopes.

57, Rue Cuvier, 5ᵉ.

Garden open every day 7.30am–8pm in summer, 8am–5.30pm in winter. Free admission.

Large greenhouses: open Wed-Mon 10am–6pm in summer, 10am–5pm in winter.

€6 for adults, €4 for children under 16, free for children under 4.

9 LEFT BANK-STYLE FUN

The **Jardin du Luxembourg** is a romantic location, but there's more… it's also a haven for kids at weekends. The older ones set up improvised football games on the paths, while the younger ones watch their boats on the large pond, ride donkey carts, leave the swings for the roundabout and generally have a ball in the large playground (paid admission, parents included). Adults who may be overwhelmed by this playground atmosphere, can escape to play a game of tennis on the municipal courts.

Entrances: Place Edmond-Rostand, Place André-Honnorat, Rue Guynemer, Rue de Vaugirard, 6ᵉ. Free admission to the garden. Opening times available on www.senat.fr

10 THE PLACE TO BE FOR BOHO KIDS

In a futuristic setting designed according to sustainable principles, your kids can have fun while contemplating the future in **Parc Martin Luther King**, laid out over four hectares. A number of playgrounds for children of all ages are arranged side by side in the middle of plant-filled and aquatic spaces: children's games, water jets, skatepark, courts for basketball and fives (handball), football pitches and even pétanque courts. On the horizon, a miniature skyline of striking buildings seemingly conquered by plants… a taste of the Paris of tomorrow.

147, Rue Cardinet, 17ᵉ. Free entry into the garden.

Opening times available at equipement.paris.fr/parc-clichy-batignolles-martin-luther-king-2817

Cycling routes

If you're planning to take your kids cycling, it's best to avoid the traffic and make use of the cycle paths where there is more green space. Here are a few routes where you don't need to worry about motorists.

FOR CHILDREN UNDER 4, THE JARDIN D'ACCLIMATATION

The **Jardin d'acclimatation** is the ideal place to start learning to ride a bike in a completely safe and car-free space. Toddlers can give cycling a try using the balance bikes and bikes with stabilizers made available to parents.
Bois de Boulogne, 16ᵉ.

FOR CHILDREN AGED 4–7: THE SEINE QUAYSIDE, LEFT BANK

Take advantage of the pedestrianized quays flanking the Seine as your first cycle routes. Stretching over 2 kilometres, the quays allow you to start with small family rides. And if the route is too long, there's always an ice cream stall, a climbing wall or giant blackboard for a pleasant distraction, making for a great day spent in one of the most beautiful spaces in the city and envy of the world.

FOR CHILDREN AGED 4–7: PARIS RESPIRE

Every Sunday and public holiday, certain streets and even whole neighbourhoods are made off-limits to motor vehicles. 'Paris Respire' (Paris breathes) gives pedestrians, skaters and cyclists free rein of the streets where motorists typically make them feel unwelcome. This is an opportunity for the whole family to enjoy a safe and tranquil bike ride, free from the smell of exhaust fumes. There are sixteen sites throughout Paris where this takes place. Traffic is banned in the Marais, Montmartre and Sentier neighbourhoods, the quays of the Right Bank and along the Canal Saint-Martin, as well as in the Mouffetard, Ranelagh and Daguerre districts. And don't forget the Bois de Boulogne and the Bois de Vincennes. Paris is open to you and invites you to enjoy the open air.

paris.fr/loisirs/se-promener-a-paris/paris-respire-et-vous

FOR OLDER KIDS COULÉE VERTE -> BOIS DE VINCENNES

For a good dose of fresh air and lush green surrounds, take the Coulée Verte, also known as the Promenade Plantée, a linear park on an old stretch of railway line in the twelfth arrondissement, The aim is to reach Lac Daumesnil, a lake in the Bois de Vincennes, and ride round it. It's also an opportunity to take a few of the paths through the woods, some of which are designed for cyclists. Then take Avenue Daumesnil and head for the Château de Vincennes. A stop will allow you to go and have a look at it (free to visit if you're under 25).

The route finishes at the Parc Floral, where your kids can burn off any leftover energy in the playgrounds.

BOIS DE BOULOGNE

If you're in the west of Paris, a good choice is a ride through the Bois de Boulogne, which has a large number of tree-lined paths. You can ride round the different lakes and water features and enjoy the cool shade under the trees without fear of cars. Make a brief stop at the Chalet des Îles, a restaurant that is a haven of peace with a terrace where you can have a drink or dinner in absolute tranquillity. Not far from there, a little to the south-west, is the Domaine National de Saint-Cloud, which also has a large number of tree-lined paths.

PARC DE LA VILLETTE -> CANAL DE L'OURCQ -> PARC DÉPARTEMENTAL DE LA BERGÈRE

As a bonus, this route leads away from Paris. Start at Parc de la Villette and simply ride along the Canal de l'Ourcq. Along the way, you'll be able to make out the Grands Moulins de Pantin complex and the building housing the Centre National de la Danse. When you reach the Parc Départemental de la Bergère, you'll have the chance to grab a bite to eat. Otherwise, the nearby Parc Henri-Barbusse offers several cycle paths.

13

Map of places to ride a bike in Paris

JARDIN MARTIN
LUTHER KING

JARDIN
D'ACCLIMATATION

PARC
MONCEA

PARC
MONCEA

SEINE
QUAYSIDE

BOIS DE
BOULOGNE

PARC JAVEL
ANDRE CITROËN

PARC
GEORGES BRASSENS

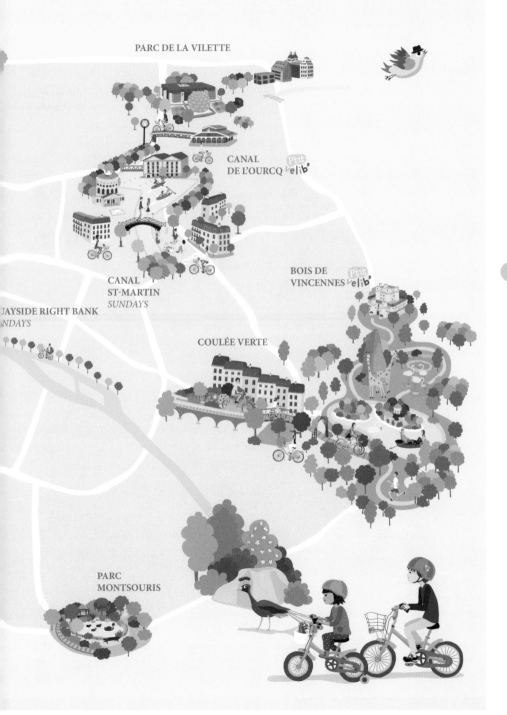

PARC DE LA VILETTE

CANAL
DE L'OURCQ *P'tit* **elib'**

CANAL
ST-MARTIN
SUNDAYS

BOIS DE
VINCENNES *P'tit* **elib'**

JAYSIDE RIGHT BANK
NDAYS

COULÉE VERTE

PARC
MONTSOURIS

Learn to ride a bike in 10 lessons

'When I get older, I'm going to use Velib', too!' the older one insists. To prepare him for being a competent urban cyclist, there's nothing better than teaching him to ride a bike as a child. Start your kids off on two wheels calmly, in a Parisian park or a suitable pedestrian area. With a few ideas on exercises for them to do, teaching them to ride will be simple and fun. Follow this guide.

16

1. GETTING USED TO A BIKE

Even before letting your child mount a bike, walking beside it while holding the handlebars is good exercise for gaining awareness of the space it takes up. A short walk will allow a child to work out how to turn to avoid an obstacle (angle, speed, distance), the room needed to do a half turn, the way the brakes work and how to allow the bike to come to a more or less full stop, and so on. And it won't take much for you to teach your child how to **mount and dismount the bike**. Ideally, this should be from the right: the bike will be between them and the traffic, and if they should lose their balance, they should also develop the reflex to fall to the right, onto the pavement, instead of to the left, onto the road. Adjust the seat to the correct height: their feet should be able to touch the ground.

2. THE BALANCE BIKE: DEVELOPING A SENSE OF BALANCE

A balance bike is a bicycle without pedals. It is a good starting point for acquiring a natural balance between holding the handlebars and applying the body weight needed in order to move straight ahead. Once this 'dynamic equilibrium' is gained, working the pedals will be child's play. This is also a way for children to skip the stabilizer stage.

Good to know: you can transform any bike into a balance bike by temporarily removing the pedals.

Learning exercises

• Encourage your child to sit on the balance bike and to walk. Little by little, they should try to take increasingly longer steps and to gradually pick up speed.

17

• At this point, the child should attempt to progressively stay off their feet and keep them up in the air for as long as possible. By stretching or bending their knees, the young cyclist is able to hold their direction. It may now be useful to raise the seat a little so that the child has to stand on tiptoes.

• **Let them find their balance** by only moving the handlebars and not using their body, which should stay quite upright. They should learn to look straight ahead or in the direction they want to go: the bike will move towards where they are looking.

• Let them practise **going round corners** with wider and tighter angles so that they realize how much space is needed to negotiate them.

• Let them become familiar with **braking**, first when stationary: by squeezing a brake lever and trying to move the balance bike forwards. Then let them push off and try to stop the bike by using the brake levers and not their feet.

3. PEDALLING AND LEARNING TO PUSH OFF

Once the basics have been learned, it's time to put the pedals back on the bike and learn to use them and to get the bike moving by pushing off without wobbling and swerving. For this to happen, good coordination is needed, as is taking the time to practise.

Mastering the pedals: on a gentle slope, let the child push off and put their feet on the pedals without looking, then teach them to pedal. The child should learn to put their feet on the pedals without looking down.

Pushing off: the safest and easiest way to do this is to have the bike between the child's legs, with one pedal brought up to its highest position, and have the child put their foot on it and give the first push.

Pedalling: encourage the child to coordinate their movements, then try to ride up a gentle slope to become aware of importance of pushing down with enough strength. A hill start is obviously trickier, especially without wobbling and swerving.

4. BRAKING

Children should learn to gauge the right amount of pressure to apply to the brakes if they are to be able to stop suddenly. To do this, they should know how to stop the bike using the back and front brakes at the same time. The rear brakes aren't effective enough to stop quickly, while if the front brakes are applied too abruptly, the front wheel risks being blocked, causing the back wheel to lift off the ground and throw the cyclist off balance. The ideal amount of pressure: 1/3 **rear and** 2/3 **front.**

Exercises

• **Controlling speed:** the adult walks or runs in front of the child on a bike; the child should adapt their speed and stopping to always keep the same distance from the adult they are following. It is a good idea to teach the child to ride slowly: more balance is required.

• **Readiness to brake:** the child rides a set course and has to stop at a landmark with prior notice given (a bench, a cross drawn on the ground, and so on) and when the adult makes a signal to stop (by whistling or holding up an arm, for instance).

5. HOLDING A COURSE

Budding cyclists should be able to ride along a set route and hold a precise course.

Following a line: the child should ride over a course with narrow stretches or very close to a hedge, or with their wheels well aligned over a straight line drawn with chalk over the ground, for example.

Changing course: give additional instructions. The child should ride towards the adult and then pass via the left or right when the adult signals by holding out their arm to the right or to the left.

Following a course: the child should follow an adult mounted on a bike, keeping a constant distance and following the adult's path as precisely as possible. Indicate that you're changing direction in advance with your arm, the goal being that they should learn to anticipate and observe their surroundings and not just stare at your back.

6. ACCURATE STEERING

It's essential that the child is able to turn wider and tighter corners at faster and slower speeds.

Zigzagging: put several objects in a line on the ground and get the child to zigzag between the objects. When the last object is reached, the child then turns round and works their way in the other direction. Bring the objects closer together to make the turns tighter, or get the child to ride faster.

Figure of eight: a variation consists of getting the child to ride a bike in a figure of eight that gets increasingly smaller. They can also ride over all the numbers from one to nine drawn on the ground.

7. LOOKING ROUND AND HOLDING OUT AN ARM

Before pushing off into traffic, it is essential that a child is able to indicate to others the direction they are going to take.

Turning the head without swerving: the memory game While getting your child to ride in a straight line, ask them as they pass you to tell you what object you have drawn on the card you're showing them. Your young cyclist should be able to look behind them (not only to the sides) without riding off course.

Holding out an arm: Simon Says on a bike To indicate that they're about to turn, a cyclist should be able to indicate their direction without riding off course. In order to train them to do so, get your learner to ride freely and imitate the movements you make: hold out your left arm horizontally, then the right vertically, and so on, without wobbling or swerving. When the child feels confident enough, play Simon Says: raise your arm to the left, touch your nose with your right hand, and so on.
Once again, the child must control their balance and hold their course.

8. FIRST EXPERIENCES IN THE CITY: ANALYSE THE SITUATION AS A PEDESTRIAN

Understanding traffic and knowing the road rules are essentials that a child needs to know if they want to gain more autonomy on city streets. Contrary to what you may believe, accidents involving young pedestrians occur more often in the presence of an adult and close to home.
Children under the age of 7 have difficulty gauging distances and speed, and find it hard to identify where a sound is coming from (left or right); and **more particularly, they think that if they can see a car, the driver of the car can also see them…**
Explain the dangers of the road: learning to cross the road is vital.

• They must walk, not run, across the road at pedestrian crossings and not turn back, and be very familiar with the drill (look left, look right, and look left again).
• If there's a traffic light, they automatically have to wait for the 'little green man', even if there's nothing coming.
Mark out routes on foot: take advantage of certain short, familiar routes to teach children aged 7 or 8 to gain autonomy. Teach them to take note of difficulties (driveways, road works, and so on), show them street signs along the route and road markings, and point out the behaviour of others round them. Speak to them about streets where cyclists are allowed to ride against the flow of traffic; show them the different sorts of cycleways and traffic lights for cyclists; and explain how cyclists can turn right only at certain intersections and for the first street on the right.
A good way to assess their progress is to suggest changing roles and to let them take you by the hand and guide you.

9. DANGERS AND BEHAVIOURS TO AVOID

Before your child sets off into the traffic, they must be completely at ease on their bike and be familiar with the additional safety rules that apply to cyclists.
Awareness of blind spots: the best way of teaching your child awareness, if you have a car, is to get them to sit in the driver's seat (in a stationary car, of course) and to check the extent of their field of vision. It's also a good way of emphasizing that one of the best ways a cyclist can protect themselves (and not only themselves) is to establish visual contact with other road users.

Pointing out bad habits: using a phone while riding, using headphones, an untied shoelace or a scarf hanging down that could become tangled in a wheel, a bag hanging from a handlebar and covering the wheel, carrying a passenger on a bicycle pannier rack, or wearing a helmet without taking the trouble to do it up or adjust it; there are so many behaviours that can prove dangerous because they show that a person is not paying attention.

10. FIRST FAMILY RIDES RIDING IN SINGLE FILE

Your child is officially considered a cyclist if they are able to push off without wobbling, ride in a straight line even at low speed, follow a specific path while turning, slowing down and braking at a precise spot, holding a straight course while holding out an arm or looking behind, and estimating and keeping a safe distance.

Until the age of 8, a child is permitted to ride at walking pace on the pavement. It is recommended that **a child under the age of 12 should not cycle alone in an urban area**; a young cyclist would have difficulties dealing with chaotic traffic and making the necessary decisions quickly. Children can use the **Velib' bike hire service for adults at the age of 14**. On your first family rides, the learner cyclist should ride behind you in single file, keeping a steady distance. Start by suggesting a route consisting of **plenty of landmarks and as many cycleways as possible**. A map of Paris cycling routes is available. You can also consider streets closed to traffic every Sunday as part of the Paris Respire programme (see p. 13). Young cyclists should learn the habit of not riding too far to the right, as there is a risk of being surprised by a car door being unknowingly opened by a driver who has just parked. In narrow streets, they should be encouraged to make full use of the roadway: if the width of the street is less than 1.5 metres, cars can't overtake. In case of heavy traffic at an intersection or if they lack confidence, tell them not to think twice about dismounting and dealing with the intersection as a pedestrian. Teach them to check their bikes well before setting off (brakes, tyres, lights).

Finally, in order to evaluate how they analyse situations, and if you feel they're seasoned enough, you can let your child ride at the front of the family team, and take their turn as the lead cyclist.

Happy cycling!

The best places
to skateboard and roller skate

There's more to life than a bike. You can take a break now and again and let your children take up another sport on wheels, or rather on small wheels: skateboarding or roller skating. Paris has many places that are suitable for skating where younger kids spend their afternoons. But they mustn't forget their elbow pads, knee pads and helmet!

PALAIS OMNISPORTS DE PARIS-BERCY / ACCORHOTELS ARENA (POPB)
The skatepark here has two levels.
The upper level consists of large ledges (solid modules for skateboarders to glide along) of all sizes, and there is an immense flat, with not a car in sight.
1, Boulevard de Bercy, 12ᵉ.

LE PETIT CLADEL
The concept behind this small skatepark in the heart of Paris is quite unusual: the entire street is dedicated to skateboarding, and to the pedestrians who share the street. To be more precise, it's actually a 'streetpark' with a ramp, ledges and a pyramid, all of which is on a really smooth flat.
Rue Léon-Cladel, 2ᵉ.

ESPACE DE GLISSE PARISIEN EGP18
Covering an area of more than 3,000 square metres, this is the largest indoor concrete skatepark in the country.
It features a permanent roof and two areas, one for beginners and the other for experienced skateboarders. EGP 18 offers a wide range of activities for general fun, starting out and serious training in roller skating, skateboarding and BMX riding.
Impasse des Fillettes, 18ᵉ.
equipement.paris.fr/espace-de-glisse-parisien 18ᵉ-egp-18-3699

ROLLER PARC JEMMAPES

This may be the smallest skatepark, but it's big on quality. Located alongside the Canal Saint-Martin, it's pleasant to give it a go in the cool of the morning, before the afternoon rush. You'll find everything you need to teach yourself a few tricks.

142, Quai de Jemmapes, 10ᵉ.

ESPACE DE GLISSE DE LA MUETTE

Spread over 750 square metres, this space is equipped for roller skates, skateboards, BMX bikes and scooters. It offers a bowl over three levels, a grind box, a ramp, two banks with pool coping and a space where you can start to learn different tricks.

52, Boulevard Lannes, 16ᵉ.
Open Mon-Sat 11am-9pm, Sun 10am-6pm.

SKATEPARK DES BATIGNOLLES

Parc Clichy-Batignolles was created on the site of the former Batignolles goods yard. Inside it you'll find the skatepark (for skateboards, roller skates and scooters). Its facilities are in stainless steel and are ideal for learning to master ledges, ramps, slides and jumps.

146, Rue Cardinet, 17ᵉ.

Just like being in the countryside

A gardener in the making

What do you mean, little Parisians don't know about nature? There's no need to spend the weekend in the Larzac to teach them about plants and the joy of growing their own vegetables. Balconies, roof terraces, courtyards, green roofs, community gardens... there are a great many places for urban agriculture in the French capital. So it's essential to teach you children about the joys of planting vegetables and watching them grow.

CENTRE FOR ORGANIC GARDENERS

Would you like to work on your green thumb? **Maison du Jardinage** is a resource centre for urban gardeners who value organic gardening methods. In addition to providing ideas and advice, the centre encourages gardening and teaches the skills needed to care for plants and to create new gardens. The centre's vegetable garden showcases a large number of species grown using organic methods. A wide selection of lessons are offered and taught by gardeners, botanists and experts in urban biodiversity on a wide range of topics.
128, Quai de Bercy, 12ᵉ. +33 1 53 66 14 00.
€6 for a 2-hour lesson

THE SCHOOL FOR PARISIAN GARDENERS

École Du Breuil offers a broad programme of lessons held at the school on Saturday mornings and at the Maison du Jardinage inside Parc de Bercy on Saturday afternoons. The programme is offered twice a year, from October to December, and from January to June. You can enrol for them throughout the year, depending on availability.

Route de la Ferme, Bois de Vincennes, 12ᵉ.
€30 for a 6-hour lesson (2 x 3 hours, Sat am)
ecoledubreuil.fr

THE HIDDEN GARDEN AT THE PARC FLORAL

The **Jardin Insolite** is a garden hidden in the midst of the Parc Floral orchard. Created in 1989, this 400-square-metre expanse is a green oasis comprising an arbour, an old greenhouse and a small shed, reminiscent of the gardens of old. A vegetable garden, fragrant garden and ornamental garden at the same time, its upkeep is in tune with natural cycles. It's surrounded by thick hedges that attract the wildlife taking part in its natural balance. There are gardeners on site to answer any questions your budding gardeners may have and can provide you with tricks and tips for organic gardening.
Parc Floral, Bois de Vincennes, 12ᵉ.
Open May–Oct, Sundays and public holidays.

JARDINS PASSAGERS AT PARC DE LA VILLETTE

Few Parisians are familiar with these gardens, a 3,000-square-metre expanse inside Parc de la Villette offering a route through and round a Mediterranean garden, fallow fields, a pond, meadow, orchard, vegetable garden, lagoon and beehives as an introduction to urban ecology and biodiversity. Adapted facilities allow both young and old to take part in the life of these gardens through a large number of educational workshops. An hour-long, free guided tour takes place on Satudays and Sundays at 5 p.m.
Open May–Sept, Sat–Sun 3–7pm. +33 1 40 03 7575
lavillette.com

25

CLOS DES BLANCS MANTEAUX GARDENS

Located in the heart of the Marais district of Paris, the garden at Clos des Blancs Manteaux holds workshops for little gardeners aged 4–7, where they are encouraged to discover, observe, sow, plant, water, harvest, decorate, create, build, draw, feel and listen. These workshops focusing on plants, nature and the environment are both fun and creative to appeal to kids.

21, Rue des Blancs-Manteaux, 4ᵉ.
+33 1 44 78 20 75.
Wed 2–3pm for 4–5 year-olds, 3.30–5pm for 6–7 year-olds. Every second Saturday, parents and children's workshop 10am–12 noon.

THE RECYCLING GARDEN

For kids aged 4 and over, the **Débrouille Compagnie** offers and introduction to urban gardening under the motto of 'recycle'. Children give new life to different materials and create useful objects for gardening, such as plant stands, scarecrows and water tanks. Spring and summer are devoted to tasks such as sowing, planting and transplanting. Autumn and winter are focused on topics related to nature (the seasons, natural cycles, biodiversity, and so on) and to revealing the secrets of making compost.

4 *ter*, Rue de la Solidarité, 19ᵉ.
+33 1 53 19 75 58.
Wed 2–4pm €10 per session. debrouille.com

Green routes in Paris: places to learn about urban ecology

In order to make our city more pleasant, and to improve our surroundings and our quality of life, there are a number of centres, establishments and places in Paris devoted to ecology. Whether promoting sustainable development, improving air and water quality or enhance the value of gardens and green spaces, each of these areas has its own set of resources. Here's overview of the environmentally minded places that make Paris nicer.

FILL UP WITH ECO-FRIENDLY IDEAS
Maison des Acteurs du Paris Durable
is the meeting place for a 100,000-strong community of Parisians who are striving every day to make Paris a greener, more caring and more pleasant place. It's a place where environmental actions and ideas can be shared, events can be publicized and other interested people can be met.

There are a large number of topics covered: waste reduction, responsible consumption, soft mobility, biodiversity, eco-design, community gardens, reducing energy use, recycling… The site contains a multi-purpose hall, three workshops and an organic garden. Events, debates, workshops, lectures and visits are held each month.
21, Rue des Blancs-Manteaux, 4ᵉ.

acteursduparisdurable.fr

GETTING TO KNOW THE PARISIAN ECOSYSTEM

Located inside Parc Floral, **Maison Paris Nature** invites ecologically minded residents of the French capital to discover the wealth of its plant and animal wildlife. Through discovery workshops held in the Butterfly Garden, this special place also raises awareness of and offers information and education on the natural treasures of the capital, which isn't made only of concrete.
Parc Floral, 12ᵉ.
paris.fr/pratique/paris-au-vert/bois-de vincennes/maison-paris-nature

LEARN TO CARE FOR OUR AIR

Maison de l'Air, located in Parc de Belleville, has a permanent exhibition on the city, its skies and atmospheric phenomena. Now that air quality is threatened by human activity, the purpose of Maison de l'Air is to explain the connections between the city's residents and its air. The air and the senses, its passengers (birds, insects, and so on), plants that release pollen and seeds into the wind, rain and fine weather are some of the subjects explained, always in an entertaining way.
27, Rue Piat, 20ᵉ.
Open Wed and Sat, Mar–Oct 1.30–5.30pm, Nov–Feb 1.30–5pm.
Free admission.

OFF TO THE FARM

Yes, Paris also has a farm. Located inside the Bois de Vincennes, **Ferme de Paris** (also see p. 55) is an educational farm that is managed in an environmentally friendly way. It is part of the Écologie Urbaine network and offers a programme of activities focusing on ecology.
On special days, visits, workshops and lectures offer a specific approach to be given to the topics dealt with. Family gardening workshops, for instance on the planting of fruit trees, are also offered at weekends.
Route du Pesage, Bois de Vincennes, 12ᵉ.
Open Sat and Sun, Apr–Sept 1.30–6.30pm, Nov–Feb 1.30–5.30pm, Nov–Feb 1.30–5pm, Mar–Oct 1.30–5pm.
Free admission.

DIVING INTO THE WATERS OF HISTORY
Located inside a former pumping station, the **Pavillon de l'Eau** is a place that offers information and raises public awareness of water-related issues. It has a permanent exhibition on the system supplying water to Paris, in addition to temporary exhibitions, children's workshops and themed video projections and meetings.
77, Avenue de Versailles, 16ᵉ.
Open Mon–Fri 10am–6pm, Sat 11am–7pm.
Free admission.

SAVE OUR CLIMATE
The **Paris Climate Agency** is an association with the goal of improving climate. It undertakes a variety of actions, among which are the promotion of energy savings, offering guidance to people who want to change their behaviour, developing renewable energies and fighting climate change. It provides particular assistance to families who want to implement energy-saving programmes in their homes.
3, Rue François-Truffaut, 12ᵉ.
Information +33 1 51 1 58 33 90 20,
Mon–Fri 10am–6pm.

29

Head for the water!

All kinds of swimming pool

Knowing how to swim is like knowing how to ride a bike; the best thing is to learn while young so you have your whole life to enjoy it. Fortunately, Paris has many swimming pools that are suited to your child's level of development, so that they can appreciate the water from an early age.

AQUAMATERNITY

Let's start by thinking about the expectant mother.
Is your well-rounded bump is weighing you down, and do you feel like a marine mammal? Head for the water and you'll find relief through aquanatal sessions. Antenatal classes held in a pool are a wonderful way to relax and calmly prepare yourself to have your baby. Aqua yoga, gentle fitness exercises and swimming make use of very slow movements in the water and can be taken up in the third month of your pregnancy. Three Parisian pools offer sessions for pregnant women to relieve stress:

Piscine Georges-Drigny
18, Rue Bochart-de-Saron, 9ᵉ.

Centre d'animation La Grange-aux-Belles 6,
Rue Boy-Zelenski, 10ᵉ.

Piscine Pontoise
17, Rue de Pontoise, 5ᵉ.

NEW SENSATIONS FOR BABY

From the age of 3 months, babies can be enrolled in baby swimming lessons at several municipal pools and bassins-école (swimming pools for students and clubs) in Paris. However, it's recommended that you wait until 6 months before taking them to the pool so that the water temperature is more suitable for them. Lessons are adapted for children up to the age of 6 to make them feel like fish in water.

BASSIN-ÉCOLE JEAN-DAME

Depending on the child's age, lessons are held on Saturdays by the Association L'Enfant d'Eau, and on Sunday mornings by Association Les Poissons Volants.
17, Rue Léopold-Bellan, 2ᵉ. lenfantdeau.fr

BASSIN-ÉCOLE DE L'ÉCOLE POLYTECHNIQUE

Lessons are held on Saturday mornings, depending on the child's age, by Association Bébés Nageurs Paris 5ᵉ.
1, Rue Descartes, 5ᵉ.
Information available at quefaire.paris.fr/fiche/65762_bebes_ nageurs

BASSIN-ÉCOLE CLER

Depending on the child's age, lessons are held on Monday and Tuesday evenings, Wednesday afternoons and Saturdays by Association Sports 7.
6, Rue Cler, 7ᵉ. sports7.fr

31

PISCINE GEORGES-RIGAL
Several sessions are offered on Saturday mornings and afternoons by the Office du Mouvement Sportif for the eleventh arrondissement.
115, Boulevard de Charonne, 11ᵉ.
oms-paris11.org

PISCINE REUILLY
For sessions are held on Saturday mornings between 8 and 10 a.m. by Association Colombes de Bercy.
13, Rue Hénard, 12ᵉ. cdbercy.free.fr

BASSIN-ÉCOLE ÉLISABETH
Sessions are held on Tuesdays and Fridays starting at 6 p.m and on Wednesdays starting at 7 p.m. by Association Femina Sport. Sessions on Wednesdays between 8.15 and 11 a.m. held by Association Aquavive. Sessions on Satudays between 3.30 and 5.30 p.m. held by the Association Vivre l'Eau. Sessions on Sundays from 9 to 11.15 a.m. held by Association Archimède. 11, Avenue Paul-Appell, 14ᵉ.
feminasport.asso.fr aquaviveetlesbebespoissons. com vivre-l-eau-paris.org archimede.asso.fr

BASSIN-ÉCOLE BIANCOTTO
Sessions held on Mondays and Fridays from 4.45 to 6 p.m., Saturdays from 8.45 to 11 a.m. and from 3.30 to 5.30 p.m., and Sundays from 8.45 a.m. to 12.30 p.m., depending on the child's age. All sessions are held by Association Nouvelle Vague.
6, Avenue de la Porte-de-Clichy, 17ᵉ.
nouvellesvagues.fr/bebe-nageur/

PISCINE HÉBERT
Sessions on Wednesdays from 8.45 to 11.15 a.m. and Saturdays from 8.30 a.m. to 12 noon, held by Association APAA.
2, Rue des Fillettes, 18ᵉ. +33 1 46 07 95 51.

PISCINE MATHIS
Sessions held by Club Les Mouettes de Paris on Tuesdays from 6.30 to 7.15 p.m. and Thursdays and Fridays from 6.15 to 7 p.m. Several sessions are held on Saturdays from 6.15 to 8.30 p.m., depending on the child's age, by Association 7ième Compagnie.
15, Rue Mathis, 19ᵉ. mouettesdeparis.com la7iemecompagnie.com

PISCINE ALFRED-NAKACHE
Several sessions are held on Saturdays between 9 a.m. and 12.45 p.m, depending on the child's age, by Association ASPL20.
4-12, Rue Dénoyez, 20ᵉ. aspl20.chez-alice.fr

BASSIN-ÉCOLE VITRUVE

Tuesdays from 5 to 6 p.m and Fridays between 4.30 and 6.45 p.m. for children aged 3–6 years. Several sessions held on Saturdays between 8.15 a.m. and 12.45 p.m., depending on the child's age. This activity is offered by Association ASPL20.
4-12, Rue Dénoyez, 20ᵉ. aspl20.chez-alice.fr

PADDLING, SPLASHING AND HAVING FUN...
PARIS WATER PARKS

Having outgrown the baby swimmer stage, the activities at water parks allow children to get the best use of a pool without their parents. Lots of toys are available to the delight of young kids: slides, floating mats and pool noodles, among others. A short 30 minutes–1 hour of aquatic joy should give your child confidence and get them ready for swimming lessons.

Piscine Paul-Valeyre
(2–8 years) 24, Rue de Rochechouart, 9ᵉ.

Piscine Château-Landon
(4–6 years) 31, Rue du Château-Landon, 10ᵉ.

Piscine Champerret
(4–6 years) 36, Boulevard de Reims, 17ᵉ.

Piscine Hébert
(4–6 years) 2, Rue des Fillettes, 18ᵉ.

Piscine Bertrand-Dauvin
(3–5 years) 12, Rue René-Binet, 18ᵉ.

Piscine Édouard-Pailleron
(with or without parents)
32, Rue Édouard-Pailleron, 19ᵉ.

Piscine Alfred-Nakache
(3–5 years) 4, Rue Dénoyez, 20ᵉ.

Piscine Georges-Vallerey
(3–5 years) 148, Avenue Gambetta, 20ᵉ.

LEARNING TO SWIM

At 6–7 years of age, your child can be enrolled for swimming lessons at swimming pools operated by Paris city council.
You just have to turn up at the pool of your choice and enrol your child with a swimming instructor for either individual or group lessons.

33

Go with the flow

When it's hot in Paris, finding a place to cool down isn't easy. Swimming pools, benches in the shade and air-conditioned shops may be a good idea, but they're often packed. However, Paris abounds with cool places where you can enjoy the warm air and cool down whenever you need to. There's nothing like getting close to water to feel its reviving coolness.

MIST SPRAY AT PLACE DE LA RÉPUBLIQUE

The newly designed Place de la République hits the spot on hot days. Next to the pavilion housing the Monde et Médias Café, a water mirror created on the ground sprays mist and jets of water when triggered. In the shade, away from the traffic and close to the terrace of a café serving cool drinks, this is the ideal spot for kids and their parents alike. **Place de la République, 3ᵉ, 10ᵉ and 11ᵉ.**

34

DANCING WATER JETS AT PARC ANDRÉ-CITROËN

Parc André-Citroën is the place to be when the heat is unbearable. 72 water jets erupt randomly over its 14 hectares of lawns, turning the esplanade into a giant shower. You'd better have swimming costumes and towels at the ready, because these jets can give you a real soaking.

2, Rue Cauchy, 15ᵉ.

MIST SPRAYS AND SEA SHELLS AT PARIS PLAGES

Every summer, sand is laid down to create beaches on the quayside of the Right Bank, the square in front of the Hôtel de Ville (city hall) and round the Bassin de la Villette. You can work on your tan while the kids build magnificent sand castles and cool off regularly under the mist sprays. Lots of activities are available for kids.

AQUATIC LANDSCAPES AT PARC MARTIN-LUTHER-KING

The former Parc Clichy-Batignolles is now a multi-faceted space, and water is present in many forms. To cool the atmosphere, there are water jets that are both aesthetic and for playing in, and there is also an ornamental pond and a settling pond, combining sustainable development and landscape.

147, Rue Cardinet, 17ᵉ.

ALONG THE TRENDY BANKS OF THE CANAL SAINT-MARTIN

The tranquil side of the city can be enjoyed on the banks of the Canal Saint-Martin, especially on Sundays when it is closed to cars. It's a place for picnics, fishing, boat rides and cycling and roller skating with the family.

BEACH GARDEN AT THE JARDIN D'ACCLIMATATION

Like cooling down by the ocean, the beach garden is a great space filled with summer fun Against a backdrop of beach huts, blue and white deck chairs are arranged in the surroundings of a wading pool with water jets. With refreshing mist sprays, rainbows created by the water jets and a flower fountain shooting jets of water… you'll stay cool, in any case.

45, Avenue du Mahatma-Gandhi, 16ᵉ.

BAMBOO GROVE AT PARC DE LA VILETTE

Notice for people walking around the nineteenth arrondissement who are too hot: make your way to Parc de la Villette, where a bamboo forest is waiting for you. To ensure that the 30 species of bamboo continue to grow, the plants receive the water that drains off the lawns and are heated by the sun.

Map of Paris water fountains

Cast off!

Paris may not be on the sea, but there are place where you can learn to sail. Sailing boats ply the waters of the ponds in Paris's parks, and sailors can learn the tricks of the trade on the city's canals.

REGATTAS IN THE PARKS OF PARIS

Sailing off to dreamland… there's nothing like a beautiful wooden sailing boat floating across the waters of a pond in a Parisian garden for kids to feel like they're miles away, and to let their imaginations run wild. Several parks in Paris hire out old-fashioned toy sailing boats. The Ville de Paris concept store (boutique.paris.fr or 29, Rue de Rivoli) also offers the opportunity to purchase a little sailing boat of your own that was designed and made in Brittany. You need only decide where its home port will be.

THE PONDS IN THE TUILERIES GARDEN

Somewhat touristy but ideal for sailing, this centrally located garden has three ponds where you can sail your toy boats in the wind that blows down the most beautiful avenue in the world towards the Louvre. What's more, your child can choose what colour sails it has.
Paris 1ᵉʳ.

THE POND IN THE LUXEMBOURG GARDENS

There's nothing smarter that taking your sailing boat to the Luxembourg Gardens. Their sails make a pretty show as they glide over the waters in the shadow of the French Senate. The Luxembourg Gardens' famous chairs allow parents to sit and listen to their children's imaginary tales of sailors and pirates.
Paris 6ᵉ.

CANAL SAINT-MARTIN

For older kids, the Canal Saint-Martin is a place where lovers of model-making congregate. At weekends it the place to go to watch remote-controlled boats zigzagging between sightseeing boats as they pass the locks.
Paris 10ᵉ, 11ᵉ.

FANCY ROWING?

You can also row a boat on the three lakes found in the Bois de Vincennes and the on the lakes in the Bois de Boulogne.

Lac Daumesnil, near Porte Dorée, is a favourite spot for people who row for pleasure. With its two suspension bridges, grotto and waterfall, it's a haven of tranquillity.
+33 1 43 28 19 20.
Open every day 9.30am–8pm.
€12 for a 1–2-person boat and €13 for a 3–4-person boat, hire for 1 hr.

Lac de Minimes is a lake dotted by three islands. After rowing a boat or canoe, why not have a bite to eat at the nearby chalet?
+33 6 86 08 01 12.
€10 for a 1–2-person boat, €12 for a 3–4-person boat, hire for 1 hr.

Lac de Saint-Mandé is probably the most interesting. Set in a valley, this lake is surrounded by winding paths, groves and streams, making it one of the most enchanting places. There you will encounter Canada geese, moorhens and various species of ducks.

The lake in the Bois de Boulogne, set into the heart of this green expanse, is a must if you want to row in Paris. Find the manager, hire a boat for a few euros and row peacefully in a setting that will make you forget all your cares.

Open every day mid-Feb–late Oct 10am–7pm.
Max. 5 people per boat.
€10 for 1 hr, €6 for 30 min (€50 deposit).

TAKE THE HELM

Have you ever dreamed of being the captain of your own ship? For the first time, a Paris-based start-up allows you to hire electric self-drive boats without the need for a permit, so you can feel what it's like to be a real sailor. Marin d'Eau Douce makes it possible for you to discover a little-known side of Paris on board small boats as you navigate the canals of northern Paris. You have access to 40 kilometres of navigable waterways on the Canal Saint-Martin, Canal de l'Ourcq and Bassin de la Villette. The boats come in three sizes: the *Ace* (5-person), *Scoop* (7-person)

and Most (11-person). Price-wise, it costs between €40 and €70 to hire a boat for 1 hour, €100 for half a day on the *Ace, and up to €280 for a whole day on the Most.* A full day's hire is about 6 hours; you just have to return the boat by sunset. To make your trip even more fun for your kids, Marin d'Eau Douce to liven the experience with games (€5): pétanque, badminton and Mölkki, among others.

Bassin de la Villette. 37, Quai de Seine, 19ᵉ.
marindeaudouce.fr

A TREASURE HUNT ON THE SEINE

If you have half a day or more to spare, board a Batobus and enter into the world of pirates. Young pirates aged 7–12 are armed with an activity booklet and have to solve riddles that will lead them to search for treasure at four iconic spots in the French capital.

At the last stop, they'll find their own personalized treasure and a tasty treat... Parents also receive a booklet with the answers to the riddles and and Paris trivia.

Tip: the best place to board is at the Eiffel Tower or Musée d'Orsay stops for the full experience.

Open every day, Sept–Mar 10am–7pm,
Apr–Aug 10am–9.30pm.
€ 16 for adults, € 10 for children under 16,
free for children under 3.

Under cover

Indoor playgrounds, bowling alleys, laser tag, climbing walls

It's raining and raining and raining... Sometimes it's easy to think the weather is purposely ruining our plans to take the kids out at the weekend or on Wednesday afternoons. Here are five ideas to solve this problem and to find something to entertain the kids.

LITTLE AMERICANS

After making your kids watch *Grease*, they dream of acting like little Americans and copying the lifestyle of Sandy Olsson and Danny Zuko. Instead of taking them to eat burgers and drink milkshakes, let them burn off energy at a bowling alley.

La Quille, 111, Rue Saint-Maur, 11ᵉ.
Bowling Champerret, 1, Rue du Caporal-Peugeot, 17ᵉ. Bowling Front de Seine, 15, Rue Gaston-de- Caillavet, 15ᵉ.

LITTLE RACING-CAR DRIVERS

The way things stand, it'll be a while before you let your kids get behind the wheel of an Autolib' hire car on the Boulevard Périphérique! So, while you wait, why not offer them the chance to play on a simulator? **La Tête dans les Nuages** is Europe's largest amusement arcade and you'll be able to let your kids loose on virtual racetracks.

5, Boulevard des Italiens, 2ᵉ.
Open every day 11–12:30am, except Wed and Sun open 10am. €2 for 1 token, €15 for 9 tokens, €30 for 20 tokens. ltdn.com

LITTLE JEDI

There's nothing like a good battle with laser guns to imagine you're in a *Star Wars* movie. There are several places in Paris that offer these activities for children over the age of 7 or 8. Prices range between €10 and €15 for a 20-minute session.

Laser Paris, 9, Rue Robert-de-Flers, 15ᵉ.
laserparis.com
Laser Game Evolution
13, Rue Ernest-Cresson, 14ᵉ.
lasergame-evolution.com

LITTLE BUILDERS

Ever higher! Using the famous Kapla wooden building blocks, kids can build the tallest skyscrapers in Paris, at least in their imagination. This activity is ideal because it's suitable for all ages, even yours. So the whole family can have fun together. Kapla also holds workshops during the school holidays.

Kapla
27, Rue de Montreuil, 11ᵉ. +33 1 43 56 13 38.
kaplacentre.com

LITTLE PRIMADONNAS

The Paris Opera offers many activities to discover what goes on backstage at this Parisian cultural landmark. Artists from certain Opera performances invite you to dance, sing and improvise with your children. You can delve into the artistic world of a producer, choreographer, singer or dancer.

Palais Garnier, Place de l'Opéra, 9ᵉ.
Opéra Bastille, Place de la Bastille, 12ᵉ.
+33 1 40 01 19 88.
operadeparis.fr

LITTLE GHOSTBUSTER

For braver children over the age of ten, **Manoir de Paris** is the spookiest place in town. Halfway between a museum and an amusement park, this haunted house covers two levels and more than 1,000 square metres with an interactive route that promises lots of excitement and real-life history. Along the route, you navigate from room to room to face a different *tableau vivant* brought to life by terribly talented actors. Vampires, executioners and zombies and other undead creatures whisper into your ear and play practical jokes on you.

18, Rue de Paradis, 10ᵉ.
Fri 6–10pm, Sat and Sun 3–7pm. €25 for adults, €20 for children. lemanoirdeparis.fr

LITTLE TARZAN

Another place for kids to overcome their fears is a climbing wall. They love the freedom to be able to climb without their parents being scared for their lives. Two indoor climbing centres in Pantin and Issy-les-Moulineaux allows children and teenagers to hone their skills in the sport through courses suited to all levels.

MurMur. 55, Rue Cartier-Bresson, 93500 Pantin.
6, Bd Garibaldi, 92130 Issy-les-Moulineaux.
murmur.fr

As a family: places for parents and children

Change your routine and go out in Paris with your kids to places devoted to early learning and strengthening family ties. That way they can have fun with new toys and you won't have to step foot in a shop.

MAISON DES PETITS AT 104

Located at Centquatre, an outstanding cultural centre in the nineteenth arrondissement, la **Maison des Petits** is a place where you and your children can express your artistic side, designed by Matali Crasset. It offers babies, children under 5 and their families spaces for listening, meeting and creating.
Near Maison des Petits, the Petit Salon is a space where you can wait to be called.
5, rue Curial, 19ᵉ. +33 1 53 35 51 21.
Open Tues–Fri 3–6pm.
Free admission, limited to 30 places, no bookings and no waiting list.

HAPPY FAMILIES

Are you dreaming of a place where you can indulge yourself while still fulfilling your role as parents? This special place lets you have a coffee in a space where you can be pampered by masseurs, hairdressers and beauticians, or visit an osteopath, physiotherapist, nutritionist, paediatrician or psychologist, and where you can focus on your career in a space set aside for work. There is a child-minding service for kids up to the age of 12 while you go about your business.
Plus, workshops are held for children (early learning, motor skills) and for parents (yoga, parenting).
5, Rue du Cloître-Saint-Merri, 4ᵉ.
+33 1 40 29 89 99.
Open Mon–Fri 8am–8pm, Sat and Sun 10am–8pm.
happyfamilies.fr

MON PETIT MK2

Are you tired of going to one Disney film after another at the cinema?

For once, think of yourselves and go and see the movie you've been dying to see. The MK2 cinema at the National Library of France takes care of minding your kids during your session. Children aged 4–10 are attended to by educational teams in a large modular space fitted out by the online concept store Smallable, with an actual mini cinema, and workshop and playing spaces that can adapt to activities as needed.

128-162, Avenue de France, 13ᵉ.

+33 1 44 67 30 88.

Open Sun 1-6.30pm.

The space can be hired for birthday parties during the week.

TOY LIBRARIES

Kid's rooms generally get overcrowded with the toys they tire of very quickly. So instead of going out to buy new toys, why not borrow some? So that kids can discover new toys without filling their cupboards, while making new friends, make the most of Paris's toy libraries. They offer play areas for people of all ages. They're special places where parents and children can share in moments of fun and relaxation. Toy librarians are there to provide assistance and advice.

Ludothèque Nautilude 2, Rue Jules-Verne, 11ᵉ. +33 6 60 59 17 80.

Ludothèque Denise-Garon 8, Square Dunois, 13ᵉ. +33 9 80 34 46 09.

Ludothèque Ludido
6 bis, Rue Hippolyte-Maindron, 14ᵉ.
+33 6 51 97 38 31.

Ludothèque Planète Jeux 68, Rue Stephenson, 18ᵉ. +33 1 42 51 71 51.

Ludothèque du Centre Social ENS 2, Rue de Torcy, 18ᵉ.
+33 1 40 38 67 29.

Ludothèque La Maison des Jeux 86-88, Rue des Couronnes, 20ᵉ.
+33 1 47 97 05 08.

45

[We show you how]

Reading

THE JOY OF READING

You must admit that of all the good intentions you have for the start of the school year, getting your kids into the habit of reading is the first one you should put into practice. And for this admirable undertaking you'll find you have the everybody's approval, from teachers to grandparents. Such rare consensus means there's even more incentive. But your offspring may be harder to convince. Why read when it's so simple and instantaneous to become engrossed by the animated world of a screen? In order to overcome the scowling, pouting and lamentations of martyrs, you'll need a few infallible strategies.

A SPECIAL MOMENT

As you probably already know, children of parents who love to read are more likely to love reading when they grow up. So read novels and news articles, and read for them. The stories you read to your kids at night are a source of shared happiness if you only read the books you also like. If you're lucky enough to have a fertile imagination, tell them stories... no child can resist that kind of magic.

However, in our busy lives, finding time for reading can be a challenge. So think about delegating the task. The CDs adapted from novels and fables by Frémeaux & Associés are outstanding. Famous actors have lent their voices and talent to breathe new life into the great literary classics... Ideal for rainy weekends and long drives. fremeaux.com

OPEN UP THEIR EARS AND EYES

Consider all the resources the Paris offers. In the Marais, **Maison des Contes et des Histoires** holds storytelling and nursery rhyme sessions for babies in its gallery space where illustrations are on display.

The whole family can also go on a guided walking tour (recommended for children aged 8 and over). On a street corner, the guide from the **Sur le Pavé la Plume** team, a literary fan, brings to life texts and heroes created by the great writers. These open-air readings allow you to discover both the places that inspired the works, and the texts and poems themselves.

La Maison des Contes et des Histoires 7, Rue Pecquay, 4ᵉ.

+33 1 48 87 04 01.

maisondescontesethistoires.com

Sur le pavé la plume

Special guided tours for families.

surlepavelaplume.com

GO TO THE LIBRARY

Paris's libraries are also an excellent resource. What a treat it is for children to have their own library cards and take out the books and comics they choose after leafing through them at length under the kind and watchful eyes of the librarians. And if the coveted book isn't available, a central database allows

it to be reserved or located at another of the city's libraries. What's more, libraries offer loads of cool activities for kids: storytelling, shows, exhibitions and workshops. *En Vue* magazine offers all the information on programmed children's activities.
paris-bibliotheques.org

GOING TO BOOKSHOPS

Children's literature is a goldmine. There are albums and stories for all tastes, and it will be a challenge to leave a good bookshop without having succeeded in tempting your little ones. **Chantelivre** is the oldest children's bookshop in Paris. It was founded in 1974 by the L'École des Loisirs publishing company. Generations of book lovers have come to revere this establishment in the Sèvres-Babylone neighbourhood. It offers a vast range of books for children and young people.

[We show you how]

Children (and their parents) can have the stories explained to them in order to make a choice; the staff are familiar with ALL the books. They give excellent advice and are patient to a fault. Book signings by authors and illustrators are organized all year round, and are an opportunity for your children to meet the people who have allowed them to dream through the pages of their favourite books.

But this bookshop isn't the alone; the city is filled with excellent bookshops, all equally active and welcoming. **L'Attrape Nuages**, in the eleventh arrondissement, combines selling books with art workshops, with evening gatherings and courses during the school holidays.

They also arrange birthday parties. **L'Ouvre-Boîte**, in the tenth arrondissement, has motivated staff members who share their discoveries and hold workshops on different topics.

Chantelivre
13, Rue de Sèvres, 6ᵉ.
Open Mon 1-7.30pm, Tues-Sat 10.30am-7.30pm.
Chantelivre.com

L'Attrape Nuages 19, Rue Pétion, 11ᵉ.
Open Tues-Sat 10am-6.30pm. attrapenuages.com

L'Ouvre-Boîte
20, Rue des Petites-Écuries, 10ᵉ.
Open Tues-Sat 11am-8pm, Sun 11am-2pm.
ouvre-boite.wix.com/librairie

A TREAT FOR BOOKWORMS

Why not kill two birds with one stone by having family brunch on a Sunday at **La Librairie**? This fun restaurant has its walls covered in shelves from which parents and kids can choose the books they fancy. Here, reading at the table is permitted. And you can even borrow the books to finish reading at home, as long as you bring them back and/or bring in other books. Enjoying good food while devouring a novel: a lovely concept of sharing to everybody's taste, from the very young to the very old.

La Librairie
2, Rue Duban, 16ᵉ. +33 1 45 20 50 23.
Open Mon-Sat for lunch and dinner,
Sun brunch 11.30am-3pm.

A SHOW FOR ENTHUSIASTS

And so that you don't forget the resolutions you made at the start of the new school year, there's nothing better than browsing round an immense 'bookshop'. Offering an insight into the fantasy world of contemporary children's literature, the **Salon du Livre et de la Presse Jeunesse** is a book fair held at exhibition centre in Montreuil from the last Wednesday in November to the following Monday. Entry is free of charge for under-18s. Give yourself several hours to wander round the fair, which celebrated its thirtieth anniversary in 2014. Besides a host of exhibitors, there is a programme of exhibitions by illustrators and art events focusing on, among others, comics, cinema, teens and digital design. You won't have time to get bored. Finally, the National Library of France's website, **La Joie par les Livres**, throughout the year offers ideas on what books to read, new publications, favourites and quality contents... no more excuses; get them reading!

Salon du Livre et de la Presse Jeunesse Espace Paris-Est-Montreuil, 128, Rue de Paris, 93100 Montreuil. salon-livre-presse-jeunesse.net lajoieparleslivres.bnf.fr

Chapter 2
Discover, learn and teach yourself

Animals

Zoos

Although Paris is dominated by humans, it's quite possible to admire and get close to our animal friends. Whether farm animals, pets, wild or aquatic animals, Paris has all sorts of spaces devoted to the animal world. The littlest ones will love them.

PETITE FERME NORMANDE
Under its thatched roofs, the **Petite Ferme Normande** at the Jardin d'Acclimatation provides a home to more than 100 animals: cattle, Suffolk sheep, Grand Noir du Berry donkeys, Flemish Giant rabbits, Senegalese goats, Cameroon sheep, chickens and roosters, along with two aurochs – also known as European bison – and even six llamas. An opportunity to discover rare domesticated species.
Bois de Boulogne, 16ᵉ.
jardindacclimatation.fr

PETS
Most kids love taking care of animals. If you haven't got a pet at home, **Petits Zanimos** offers your children the chance to look after a collection of them: butterflies and other insects in vivariums, rabbits and guinea pigs, cats and friendly parakeets, among others. Their task is to feed and look after them.
25, Rue de Turin, 8ᵉ.
€ 15 for 1 hr, € 30 for 1/2 day.
lespetitszanimos.fr

MÉNAGERIE DU JARDIN DES PLANTES
Opened in 1794, this is one of the oldest zoos in the world. Most of its 1,800 occupants are small and medium-sized species and endangered species. Among them are red pandas, snow leopards, Arabian oryxes, orangutans and giant tortoises from the Seychelles. So many rare and beautiful animals! The daily programme at the Jardin des Plantes includes workshops that little nature and animal lovers will adore. For instance, you can choose the 'Mercredis des Curieux' (Wednesdays for the curious) workshop, where kids are taught to take care of the zoo animals and to get to know the plants. The 'Art et Éveil au Jardin' (art and an introduction to the garden) workshop has children making original artworks using plants and flowers in every colour.
57, Rue Cuvier, 5ᵉ.
+33 1 40 79 37 94.
Admission €13, €9 for children aged 4–16, free for children under 4.

PARC ZOOLOGIQUE DE PARIS
Run by the Muséum National d'Histoire Naturelle, this Paris zoo has been turned into a place for people to gain awareness of nature. This zoo has been totally modernized to keep up with the changing times, and is also a centre for conservation and animal welfare, and a place for science and research. It is home to 1,000 animals, of which there are 74 species of birds, 42 species of mammals and 21 of fish.
53, Avenue de Saint-Maurice, 12ᵉ.
Open Mon–Fri 10am-6pm, Sat and Sun 9.30am-7.30pm in summer, and Mon-Sun 10am-5pm in winter. Admission €22 for adults, €16.50 for 12–25-year-olds,
€14 for children aged 3-11 years.
parczoologiquedeparis

GRANDE GALERIE DE L'ÉVOLUTION

Does your child love animals and their history? Then visit the Grande Galerie de L'Évolution at the Muséum National d'Histoire Naturelle. In this vast hall, you'll find 7,000 stuffed specimens in spectacular arrangements, such as a tiger clinging to an elephant's back under a hail of euphoric monkeys coming down from the ceiling. The second level houses an exhibition on human impact on nature, while the third level is devoted to endangered species.

36, Rue Geoffroy-Saint-Hilaire, 5ᵉ.
Open every day, except Tues. Oct–Mar
10am–5pm, Apr–Sept 10am–6pm.
Entry €3, €1 for 4–25-year-olds,
free for children under 4.
mnhn.fr

LE CAFÉ DES CHATS

What could be a better way of getting warm than with a heater? And if the heater purrs? Even better. Here you can pet friendly cats on your knees as you drink your cup of hot chocolate. Inspired by Japanese cat cafés (Neko coffees), one Parisian woman decided to open her own, for her customers' well-being, in the heart of the Marais. Felines and their purring are have anti-stress qualities for us humans.

16, Rue Michel-le-Comte, 3ᵉ. Open Tues–Sun
12 noon–10.30pm.

Off to the farm

Fancy a dose of nature to let the kids roll around in the hay, see farm animals and jump about in the mud in their wellies? The Paris region (and the city itself) has a wealth of agricultural oases where a walk or even an overnight stay can be beneficial. Whether for a day or a night, you can visit small farms in the Île-de-France region.

URBAN: FERME DE PARIS

A must for young nature-loving Parisians, **Ferme de Paris** (also see p. 28) is a farm that managed in tune with the seasons and using organic farming methods. Cows, goats, sheep, pigs, chickens and rabbits live side by side, and the land is divided into fields and meadows. The orchard has a collection of different fruit trees, while the vegetable garden is filled with a large range of vegetables, herbs and medicinal plants.

**Route du Pesage, Bois de Vincennes, 12ᵉ.
Open Sat and Sun 1.30–6.30pm.**

OUT OF THE ORDINARY: ESPACE NATURE DE LA PÉPINIÈRE DU CREUX-DU-CHÊNE

Located in a small village on the River Marne, this farm produces ornamental shrubs and fruit trees. There are two options available if you want to spend the night: bring your own camping equipment or hire one of the unusual lodgings on offer (such as tree houses and caravans). With a botanical trail, fitness circuit and fishing activities, among others, you can even ride a dog sled on wheels. An educational space comprising an orchard, vegetable garden and plant nursery offer you a chance to spend half a day or even longer periods learning about nature.

16 *bis*, Grande-Rue, 77440 Tancrou.
Getting there by public transport:
Transilien suburban rail (1 hr) to Lizy-sur-Ourcq, then bus 41 to Tancrou (30 minutes).
Open Apr–Oct.
camping-insolite-chiendetraineau-77.com

GOURMET: FERME DE LA RECETTE

Between Melun and Montereau, a world away from the hum of the city, here is a farm to tantalize your taste buds. Large cultivated fields, meadows and forests welcome your family to stay in the middle of nature. You'll be enjoy the produce grown on the farm and dishes for which the place is famous, such as shallot and beef pie, sautéed farm-raised beef with Seine-et-Marne beer, guinea fowl with brie cream. A mouth-watering treat for the kids. Accommodation is available in one of three guest rooms or you can hire the holiday cottage for a bit more independence.

3, Rue du Moulin, Échou, 77830 Échouboulains.
Getting there by public transport: R train to Montereau, then bus 06 to Libération, Échouboulains.
fermedelarecette.com

REMOTE: FERME D'ORSONVILLE

Built in 1882 and located inside the Parc Naturel Régional du Gâtinais Français, Ferme d'Orsonville is a renovated farm in the historic Brie region. Covering a huge area of more than 224 hectares with meadows and woods, you can hunt game birds in groups or individually. Wheat, barley, rape, broad beans and triticale are some of the crops grown on the farm.

77190 Villiers-en-Bière.
Getting there by public transport: R train to Bois-le-Roi, or RER train to Melun, then by taxi.
ferme-orsonville.fr

HISTORICAL: FERME DU COLOMBIER

In the small rural village of Coulomnes, in the historic Brie region, three cleverly decorated guest rooms created in an old granary will allow you to have a most relaxing stay. The fortified tower was turned into a dovecote (colombier) in 1730 and has 3,426 pigeon holes and a double revolving ladder. The couple who own the farm grow cereals, broad beans, flax and hemp.

24, Place de l'Église, 77580 Coulommes.
Getting there by public transport: P train to
Coulommiers, then bus 03 in the direction
of Gare de Meaux to Coulommes.
ferme-du-colombier.com

DAIRY: FERME DE VILTAIN

Start your visit to this farm in the stables
with the milking of the cows. This is a time
kids will find special and unforgettable.
You can then sample home-made yoghurts
and fresh cheese, milk and cultured milk
products, desserts and milk jam, and buy
some to take home. You can also discover
local dishes at Ferme de Viltain.
Chemin de Viltain, 78350 Jouy-en-Josas.
Getting there by public transport: N train
direction Gare de Dreux-Gare de Versailles-
Chantiers, then bus L in the direction
of Val-d'Albian-Villeras to Central PTT,
then a 16-min walk.
viltain.fr

THE ORCHARD: FERME DE GALLY

If you'd like to fill your kitchen with quality
seasonal fruits and vegetables grown in the
Île-de-France region, then Ferme de Gally is
the place to go. You'll be lent a wheelbarrow
and given a map of the farm, and you are
left to pick your own. Ferme de Gally also
offers educational activities and workshops
for kids.
Rue du Docteur-Vaillant, 78210 Saint-Cyr-l'École.
Getting there by public transport: RER C train
direction in the direction of Gare de
Saint-Quentin-en-Yvelines to Saint-Cyr,
then a 15-minute walk.
ferme.gally.com

AND FERME DU LOGIS

It's also fun to pick fruits and vegetables
as you please here, and then have a family
meal. The novelty lies in the fact that
Ferme du Logis also turns its fruits into
delicious sorbets, jams and preserves,
and *pâtes de fruits*.
78580 Jumeauville.
Getting there by public transport: J train
in the direction of Mantes-la-Jolie to
Épone-Mézières, then bus 10 to Jumeauville.
+33 1 30 42 61 27. / lafermedulogis.com

ÉLEVAGE LA DOUDOU

You can spend your day imitating
the animals in Cheptainville. 60 cute goats,
a few dairy cows, horses, donkeys, rabbits
and poultry will be expecting you. Guided
tours of the farm and farming museum (€5)
are organized and you can also buy meat
there before heading back to Paris.
8, Chemin du Cimetière, 91630 Cheptainville.
Getting there by public transport: RER C train
to Marolles-en-Hurepoix, then bus 1002 to École,
Cheptainville, then a 5-min walk.
la-doudou.com

On the trot

If there's one sport that's stayed popular generation after generation, it's horse-riding. It's what little princesses and knee-high cowboys dream of. All over Paris there are places where you can make their dreams come true. So giddy-up and off you go to the green spaces of Paris.

PARIS PONEYS AT PARC DE CHOISY

Very popular with kids, your little ones will love this riding school in Parc de Choisy. Free entertainment and demonstrations with ponies are offered for Parisians aged 3–14. They explain the professions that use horses and how to care for animals, and offer an introduction to riding, trick riding demonstrations, first contact with ponies for children, and equestrian team sports. Lessons are also offered for children up to the age of 14.

Open every day, 45-min lessons for children aged 7–14.

Sun 10.30am–12 noon, first contact with ponies for children under 7.

PONY RIDES

As a first step to the art of horse-riding, pony rides are available for children in the Bois de Vincennes (near Lac de Saint-Mandé), the Bois de Boulogne (near the lower lake), in Parc Buttes-Chaumont, Parc Monceau, Parc Montsouris, Parc Georges-Brassens and in the Jardin du Luxembourg.

Wed, Sat, Sun and school holidays.
€3.50 per ride.
animaponey.com

SUNDAYS ON THE TROT

During April and May, Paris's Longchamp and Auteuil racecourses open their doors free of charge to the public on Sunday afternoons to offer shows featuring horses, sporting contests, medieval-style jousts, descendants of cavalrymen arriving from the Wild West and falconry displays from the hands of horsemen from the East.
dimanchesaugalop.com

EQUESTRIAN ART

Founded in 2003 by **Bartabas** in the Great Stables of the Palace of Versailles, the **Académie Équestre de Versailles** is a unique equestrian ballet company that combines classical dressage with other disciplines such as fencing, dance, singing and *kyudo* (traditional Japanese archery).

Dressage events and sessions are offered all year round, which you can attend before going on to visit the royal stables.
Avenue Rockefeller, 78000 Versailles.
acadequestre.fr

For children who love horses and poetry, **Théâtre Équestre Zingaro** puts on outstanding shows every year.
176, Avenue Jean-Jaurès, 93300 Aubervilliers.
bartabas.fr

Like a fish in water

The sea is rather far from Paris, but there's nothing to stop you from acquainting your kids with an aquatic environment and its plant and animal life. Whether at the end of a fishing line or in a glass tank, fish hold great fascination for children. To satisfy their urge for aquatic diversion, there are many ways to discover the creatures living in the waters of Paris, France and the world.

AQUARIUM DE PARIS

Located by the Eiffel Tower, this aquarium showcases the life found in the waters off the French mainland and its overseas territories. From the English Channel to Polynesia, from the Mediterranean to New Caledonia, by way of the Seine, the 43 tanks at the Aquarium de Paris stir kids' dreams of diving among sharks and small, brightly coloured fish.

5, Avenue Albert-de-Mun, 16ᵉ.
+33 1 40 69 23 23.
Open every day 10am–7pm.
€ 20.50 for adults, €16 for children aged 13–17, €13 for children aged 3–12, free for children under 3.
cineaqua.com

AQUARIUM DE LA PORTE DORÉE

This beautiful aquarium showcases the waters of tropical latitudes, where you can discover the life of those exotic regions. The 5,000 animals from 300 different species are the best way for children to take part in safeguarding biodiversity. And in order to satisfy their urge for adventure, the Aquarium de la Porte Dorée features a 135-square-metre terrarium that is home to fearsome crocodiles and alligators, and another terrarium for the much cuter tortoises.

293, Avenue Daumesnil, 12ᵉ.
+33 1 53 59 58 60.
Open Tues–Fri 10am–5.30pm,
Sat and Sun 10am–7pm.
€5 for adults, €3.50 4–25-year-olds, free for children under 4.
aquarium-portedoree.fr

SEA LIFE

Sea Life is an aquarium where you can discover the riches of the marine world and how important it is to protect them. Tanks have amazing viewing areas and are perfectly suited to young children, offering a panorama of different ecosystems, such as coral reefs, the Amazon and the deep sea.

14, Cours du Danube, 77200 Marne-la-Vallée.
+33 1 60 42 33 66.
Open every day 10am–5.30pm.
€17.50 for adults, €13.90 for children aged 3–11, free for children under 3.
visitsealife.com

STREET FISHING

There's no need to drive for miles in order to take up your fishing rod. In fact, the Canal Saint-Martin, Canal de l'Ourcq and the Seine abound in all sorts of fish.

Whether you use a fly or live bait, fishing, and particularly catch-and-release, have become the flavour of the month.

Far from being uncool, fishing has inspired its enthusiasts with different ideas: street fishing, lessons for beginners, competitions… Fishing is now a popular sport with young and old, and Paris makes a great playing field. Eco-friendly fishing is the motto by which French Touch Fishing operate. Awareness of the importance of wildlife has led these guys to safeguard it through the practice of catch-and-release. Fish are systematically unhooked and returned to the water after capture. Their fishing school teaches children modern fishing techniques, including how to choose their bait according to the fish that live in the water, and the advantages of catch-and-release fishing. This sharing of street fishing culture takes place every Wednesday at noon.

3, Rue Legouvé, 10e. +33 9 54 58 94 09. frenchtouchfishing.fr

Science and technology

A scientist in the making

Does you child love reading **Science & Vie Junior** *and conducting scientific experiments? Broaden their scientific mind and learning by taking them to the different exhibition spaces in Paris that promote the sciences.*

CITÉ DES SCIENCES ET DE L'INDUSTRIE

The Cité des Sciences et de l'Industrie in Parc de la Villette specializes in promoting the culture of science and technology, and is an ideal choice for kids of all ages. It also has a space dedicated to children aged 2–12, with permanent and temporary exhibitions. The Cité des Enfants is a play space that allows children to do experiments and begin to discover the world. Open to infants from the age of two, the place is divided into five themed spaces. An excellent way for them to develop their identity, handle objects, explore space, observe scientific phenomena and, above all, play. Older kids (5–12 years) also have their own space. They can run and measure their speed, test their balance, change their appearance, write in Chinese, generate enough energy to power a television set… in short, a programme to make them even more inquisitive and knowledgeable than they already are.

30, Avenue Corentin-Cariou, 19ᵉ.
+33 1 40 05 70 00.
Open Tues–Sat 10am–6pm, Sun 10am–7pm.
Admission €9.
cite-sciences.fr

PALAIS DE LA DÉCOUVERTE

The Palais de la Découverte is another mecca for budding Einsteins. Inventions of all kinds are exibited here, from astrophysics to chemistry by way of mathematics and biology. Temporary exhibitions are held regularly on the topics

of global warming, extraordinary natural phenomena and to pay tribute to scientists who have changed the course of history. In order to stimulate the curiosity of little scientists, chemistry, maths and biology are given as fun workshops, enough to make theory-based disciplines tangible and entertaining.
Avenue Franklin-Delano-Roosevelt, 8ᵉ.
+33 1 56 43 20 20.
Open Tues–Sat 10am–6pm, Sun 10am–7pm.
Admission €9.
palais-decouverte.fr

MUSÉE DES ARTS ET MÉTIERS
The Musée des Arts et Métiers is considered to be one of the world's oldest museums of industrial design and technology. Its history is closely connected to that of the Conservatoire National des Arts et Métiers (CNAM), the institution of higher education of which it forms a part. Discover the museum's collection as a family on your own, on a family tour, or through practical workshops held there. Every Sunday at 11 a.m, guided family tours are held for parents and children aged 7–12.

60, Rue Réaumur, 3ᵉ. +33 1 53 01 82 00.
Open Tues–Sun 10am–6pm, open until 9.30pm on Thurs. Admission €6.50, free for under-25s.
arts-et-metiers.net

EXPLORADÔME
The slogan of this interactive museum devoted to the sciences, multimedia and sustainable development is 'forbidden not to touch'. Children aged 4 and over are welcomed into a 1,000-square-metre space in Vitry-sur-Seine. Exploradôme is also a multimedia space where the public, no matter what age, is invited to learn, put into practice or develop their knowledge of new technologies.
18, Av. Henri-Barbusse, 94400 Vitry-sur-Seine.
+33 1 43 91 16 20.
Open Mon–Sat 10am–6pm, Sun 1–6pm. Admission €6, €4.50 for 4–18-year-olds, €19 for a family of 4 people.
exploradome.fr

Little geeks

From a very early age, our children seem to surf the Internet with surprising ease. They steal our smartphones and tablets before they even know how to read or write. So, in order to turn this craving into a strength for our little ones, let's encourage them to delve further into the digital world: not to make them simple online consumers, but to pave their way to becoming players, future content producers, so that their ease can be transformed into knowledge.

FIRST DIGITAL FORAY

Through a toy library specializing in video games and exhibitions showcasing computer culture, **Gaîté-Lyrique** is the ideal place to introduce kids to the digital world. Workshops teach the whole family how to make a computer, write your first line of computer code or invent stories in augmented reality. The topics covered by the workshops change throughout the year together to match the exhibitions. Whatever you make of it, this place always makes parents and children happy.

3 *bis*, Rue Papin, 3ᵉ. +33 1 53 01 52 00.
Open Tues–Fri 2–8pm, Sat and Sun 11am–7pm.
Admission €7.50, €5.50 for under-25s.
gaite-lyrique.net

LEARN TO PROGRAM

Any expert will tell you that learning a computer language in the coming years will be as important as speaking a foreign language or mastering mathematics. There's even talk of adding this subject to the baccalauréat curriculum. Therefore, it's important that from a very early age children are taught to program computers and to invent their own computer games, made possible through weekly programming workshops and courses.

Magic Makers workshops show children how to invent their own characters and to program in order to bring their story to life. Programming is accompanied by 'unplugged' manual activities such as role play, so kids become aware of the frontier between the virtual world and real life.

Weekly workshops target children over the age of 8. They last an hour and a half and are held every day in the eighth, ninth,

65

thirteenth and fifteenth arrondissements. Courses are also organized for the school holidays. There are also different scheduled events, such as discovery workshops and family workshops.
Courses cost €160, weekly workshops cost €200 for 3 months. magicmakers.fr

FROM VIRTUAL TO REAL

After learning to program, why not take advantage of this knowledge to influence the real world, by using this ease with computers to create things? Fab labs, which are springing up in Paris, allow anybody to design objects with computers using the different machines available: 3D and vinyl printers, computer-controlled milling machines, laser cutters, thermal presses, circular saws and much more. Bring your children and meet the builders of the future.

Carrefour numérique²
Cité des sciences et de l'industrie. 30, Avenue Corentin-Cariou, 19ᵉ.
+33 1 40 05 80 00.
cite-sciences.fr

Le Petit FabLab de Paris 156, Rue Oberkampf, 11ᵉ.
+33 1 77 16 48 58.
lepetitfablabdeparis.fr

Draft
12, Esplanade Nathalie-Sarraute, 18ᵉ.
+33 9 81 01 02 09.
ateliers-draft.com

Halloween

Now a permanent fixture on out calendars, this Anglo-Saxon celebration has everything kids love. On the eve of the All Saints' Day holiday, the streets of Paris are overrun with little monsters and witches. We show you how to enjoy the thrill with your family.

And when the Anglo fever takes over, it's also a good time to take stock of little sorcerers' language skills. Courses, games and sporting and artistic activities – any means is good to teach the language of Shakespeare from the earliest age. There is a vast offering in Paris and it's never to early to learn. We give you a few pointers.

[We show you how]

CELEBRATING HALLOWEEN

There are a great many ways to celebrate Halloween. Theme parks (Parc Astérix, Disneyland, and so on) put on terrifying offerings; the Hard Rock Café is opened to kids for a diabolical time filled with entertainment (Sunday before and after Halloween). Enchantment also takes over the **Stade de France**: to haunt the areas usually off limits to the public at this legendary stadium on Halloween night, make a booking on the stadefrance.fr website.

It's also a time for older ones (children over the age of ten) to head for **Manoir de Paris** (see address on p. 43), which opened in 2011 with interactive shows that recreate Parisian legends, such as the Phantom of the Opera and the Hunchback of Notre-Dame. A theatrical adventure to send shivers down your spine!

To get a fright while surrounded by wolves and deer (prudently kept in enclosures inside the park), **Château de Thoiry** holds events suited to different ages: murder parties for the older kids, and night walks for the younger ones to hunt for ghosts and witches. Château de Thoiry +33 1 34 87 49 26. thoiry.net/chateau.php

Parc Zoologique de Paris offers free activities and guided tours for younger and older kids during all the school holidays, while on Halloween the tour takes in the most frightening creatures, including snakes, tarantulas and vultures.
Online bookings and fast-track tickets: parczoologiquedeparis.fr

Bateaux Parisiens also have special Halloween cruises in which boats are turned into playgrounds for little monsters and witches while their parents admire the landmarks of Paris.
bateauxparisiens.com

Traditionally, artisans and shopkeepers at **Place de la Nation** join together to offer children face-painting and sweets.

Cueillette du Plessis
In October, winter squash fair and pumpkins for children to carve.
D20 - Route de Lumigny, 77540 Lumigny.
+33 1 64 07 71 41.
Open Mon–Fri 9am–12.30pm and 2–7pm, Sat and Sun 9am–7pm.

Warning! Vampires, witches, ghosts and scary monsters awaken on the night of Halloween and play nasty tricks. You'll have to find a scary costume and have the family ready with tricks and treats. To help with this, refer to the addresses given on p. 114.

PICK A PUMPKIN
Americans decorate pumpkins by removing the flesh and seeds, carving them and putting a candle inside to make a scary face. Gourmets make use of the seeds: cleaned, sun-dried and roasted in an oven pre-heated to 180ºC for 15 minutes, they make an excellent energy snack. And so that nothing is wasted, the flesh is made into an invigorating soup. No one can resist the pleasure of picking vegetables before winter comes, to get that precious pumpkin. cuisineamericaine-cultureusa.com/mode-demploi-comment-faire-une-citrouille-pour-halloween/

Cueillette de Cergy-Puiseux-Pontoise
Don't forget to bring bags and baskets.
A15, Exit 13, Route de Courcelles, 69
95650 Puiseux-Pontoise.
+33 1 34 46 11 21.
Open every day 9.30am–7.30pm, except Mon
2–6pm.

Cueillette de la Croix-Verte
To make it easier to get there, you can join a carpooling service.
Route de Viarnes, 95570 Attainville. +33 1 39 91
05 31.
Open every day 9am–7.30pm, except Mon 2–6pm.

Ferme de Gally, Ferme du Logis and Cueillette de Viltain (see p. 57 for addresses).
Even more farms where you can pick your own fruit and vegetables on chapeaudepaille.fr

[We show you how]

INTRODUCTION TO ENGLISH
When learning English becomes child's play!

ENGLISH FOR BABIES
Les Petits Bilingues
Workshop packages for children of all ages
(from 6 months) or lessons throughout
the year and school holiday courses.
One telephone number: +33 820 58 58 00,
and several centres:
République, 37, Boulevard Saint-Martin, 3ᵉ.
Parmentier, 19, Rue Pasteur, 11ᵉ. Saint-Antoine,
19, Rue Crozatier, 12ᵉ.
Plaisance, 141, Rue Raymond-Losserand, 14ᵉ.
Commerce, 26, Villa de la Croix-Nivert,15ᵉ.
Étoile, 8, Rue des Colonels-Renard,17ᵉ.
Batignolles, 41, Rue Truffaut, 17ᵉ.

ENGLISH BY PLAYING
Le Bus Bilingue
Hour-long play sessions in groups for
3–11 year olds with English-speaking
carers. Find a small group near your home,
or organize your own workshop.
+33 6 01 73 31 74.
Info@busbilingue.com

ENGLISH BY SINGING
Kidjam
An introduction to singing and music from
3 months, based on Dalcroze Eurythmics
(forming natural associations between
body movement and movement in the
music), among others. A pianist or guitarist
accompanies each jam session. English is
introduced using simple musical phrases,
very slowly. Courses also open to children
with special needs.

Espace Saint-Martin, Salle Saint-Alexis 11,
Rue du Docteur-Roux, 15ᵉ. info@kidjam.fr

ENGLISH ON STAGE
Centre d'Animation Arras
Discovering English through theatre,
for children aged 7–11, for 3–6 year olds
using nursery rhymes and toys.
Centre d'Animation Arras
48, Rue du Cardinal-Lemoine, 5ᵉ.
+33 1 44 32 03 50.

STORYTELLING IN ENGLISH
The **American Library in Paris** offers a story
hour for the brightest and most bilingual
kids, aged 3 and over.
10, Rue du Général-Camou, 7ᵉ.
+33 1 53 59 12 60.
americanlibraryinparis.org

CREATIVE ENGLISH
Bilingual drawing course that teaches kids
to draw while speaking English.
Centre d'Animation Les Halles-le Marais
Forum des Halles level –3, 6-8, Pl. Carrée, 1ᵉʳ.
+33 1 40 28 18 48.

ENGLISH BY WIGGLING
Gymboree
A bodily approach to language, to introduce
kids to English and let off steam, for children
aged 1–6.

Gymboree Paris Aquaboulevard
4, Rue Louis-Armand,15ᵉ.
Gymboree Paris Jardin d'Acclimatation Bois
de Boulogne, 16ᵉ.
+33 1 40 71 61 60.

ENGLISH THROUGH SPORT
Club Atheon
This club offers children aged 7–15 courses
for learning or perfecting English in small
groups in the morning. Afternoons are
devoted to sport (climbing, tennis, dance,
and so on). You can also play baseball
throughout the year or as part of a course.
Stade Jean-Bouin
26, Avenue du Général-Sarrail, 16ᵉ.
+33 7 61 74 3103 or +33 6 98 0016

ENGLISH-SPEAKING BABYSITTING
SERVICE
Le Répertoire de Gaspard
Individual or shared child minding
at home with an English-speaking babysitter.

While tending to your child's everyday
needs, the experienced babysitter will
supervise different activities for
a recreational linguistic immersion.
Custom packages: full week, full day
or half-day, during school holidays or
throughout the year, the choice is yours.
+33 1 47 20 49 48.
lerepertoiredegaspar

And also:
Babylangues Paris-le Marais 19, Rue Pavée, 4ᵉ.
+33 811 620 812.

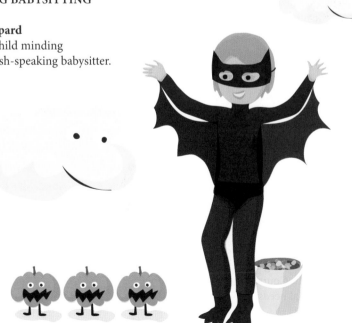

Little tourists

Once upon a time in Paris

Experience the history of Paris! From the Arènes de Lutèce, to the medieval foundations of the Louvre and the Musée de Cluny, Paris abounds in places that show the vestiges of a history rich in twists and turns. To get to know Paris and its history like the back of your hand, follow the guide.

PARIS IN ROMAN TIMES
ARÈNES DE LUTÈCE
The Gallo-Roman amphitheatre built in the first century AD was the most beautiful and magnificent in all of Gaul. The Arènes de Lutèce is all that remains of the huge structure – capable of holding more than 12,000 spectators – which was the venue for gladiatorial combats, wild animal hunts and the staging of plays. The arena can be accessed through the building at 49 Rue Monge, via Rue de Navarre and through Square Capitan on Rue des Arènes.
49, Rue Monge, 5ᵉ.
Open every day 8am–5.45pm in winter and until 9pm in summer.

CARRIÈRES DE MONTMARTRE
These quarries dating from Gallo-Roman times provided the material used to make the finest and most famous plaster of all, plaster of Paris. Today a commemorative plaque set on a wall in Square Louise-Michel at the northern end of Rue Ronsard marks what was the entrance to the quarries. Place Saint-Pierre now occupies their place.
Place Saint-Pierre, 18ᵉ.

PARIS IN THE MIDDLE AGES
TOUR SAINT-JACQUES

Standing alone in the middle of Paris's first public garden, Tour Saint-Jacques is the only remaining vestige of the church of Saint-Jacques-de-la-Boucherie.
Built in the sixteenth century, this bell tower stands 54 metres in height, and after ten years of restoration works, it can now be visited. A magnificent view of Paris can be had from the roof.
39, Rue de Rivoli, 4ᵉ.

THE MEDIEVAL FOUNDATIONS OF THE LOUVRE

Recent restoration works on the Cour Carré courtyard and construction of the pyramid have allowed a series of archaeological excavations to take place: the moat, foundations and base of the keep of the old castle were discovered. During your visit you can walk inside the moat of the medieval castle, round the base of the keep and along the moat built by King Charles V.
99, Rue de Rivoli, 1ᵉʳ.
Open every day, except Tues, 9am–6pm, Wed and Fri open until 9.45pm.
louvre.fr

ARCHIVES NATIONALES

The Archives Nationales have kept all the records of the principal institutions of the French state since the Middle Ages. The **Musée de l'Histoire de France** is also found at the same address.

The history of the archive began in 1194 when, after an attack by the English near Vendôme, King Philippe Auguste fled, leaving behind the accounts and records he would always carry with him. He then decided to set up a royal archive at the Louvre, forerunner of the Archives Nationales created by the French Revolution in the Hôtel de Soubise.
60, Rue des Francs-Bourgeois, 4ᵉ.
Open Mon–Fri 10am–5.30pm, Sat and Sun 2–5.30pm.

MUSÉE DE CLUNY

Explore the collections housed in this museum specializing in the Middle Ages and covering a thousand years of art. This exceptional complex combines two impressive buildings, the Roman baths of Lutetia, built at the end of the first century AD, and the town house (*hôtel*) once owned by the abbots of Cluny that dates from the late fifteenth century.
6, Place Paul-Painlevé, 5ᵉ.
Open every day, except Tues, 9.15am–5.45pm.
Admission €8 with audioguide.

HÔTEL DE SENS

As you walk through the Marais district, you'll no doubt come across this building that looks like something out of the Middle Ages. It houses the **Bibliothèque Forney**, a library whose collections are devoted to the decorative arts, arts and crafts, fine arts, fashion and design.
1, Rue du Figuier, 4ᵉ.
Open Tues–Sat 1–7pm.
Admission €6, reduced rates €4 and €3.

Journey to the centre of the Earth

By walking round Paris, you and your children will get to know the city well from the outside, but do you know it from the inside? Because even in the depths, there's a life and history that few people know about. The most fearless among you will be able to penetrate into the bowels of the Earth in a number of ways. Discover underground Paris…

THE CATACOMBS

Under the cobblestones of Paris there has been a second city (or near enough) since ancient times, which consists of a hundred or so underground galleries, popularly known as catacombs. A maze with a total length of 350 kilometres winds its way under a large part of the Left Bank and under certain parts of the Right Bank. Starting out as underground quarries, the catacombs were turned into an ossuary at the end of the eighteenth century, and today they are a museum.

Close to 300,000 visitors enter into the mysterious catacombs and quarries of Paris every year.

1, Avenue du Colonel-Henri-Rol-Tanguy, 14ᵉ.
+33 1 43 22 47 63.
Open Tues–Sun 10am–8pm. Admission €10, €8 for under-26s. catacombes.paris.fr

THE SEWERS OF PARIS

Did you know that Paris has the most extensive sewerage network, and the best suited to the demands of public health? Enter the bowels of the city for a tour covering the period from ancient times to the era of Belgrand, the nineteenth-century engineer who designed the present-day network. Inside the underground galleries, you learn about the water cycle and the work done by sewer workers. It's an opportunity to explore a small portion of the 2,500-kilometre network. The entrance is under the Pont de l'Alma bridge (seventh arrondissement). The streets of Paris were first paved around the year 1200 by King Philippe Auguste and a gutter was built in the middle to drain them. A vaulted sewer with masonry walls was built in 1370 under Rue Montmartre to the Ménilmontant stream.

Opposite 93, Quai d'Orsay, 7ᵉ.
+33 1 53 68 27 81.
Open Sat–Wed 10am–5pm.
Admission €4.40, €3.60 for children under 16.

75

LA CRYPTE ARCHÉOLOGIQUE DU PARVIS NOTRE-DAME

Displaying the archaeological finds discovered during a series of excavations made between 1965 and 1970, the archaeological crypt under the square in front of the cathedral of Notre-Dame de Paris provides a unique view of the urban and architectural development of l'Île de la Cité, the island that forms the historic centre of Paris. You'll find vestiges of a quay from the port of Lutetia, the Gallo-Roman public baths, a fourth-century enclosure wall, the basement of the old chapel of the Hôtel-Dieu hospital, medieval remains of the rue Neuve-Notre-Dame, foundations of the medieval foundlings hospice and part of the sewers built by Baron Haussmann. The crypt brings to life one of the oldest districts in Paris and shows how, after more than 2,000 years, the city has never ceased to rebuild over itself. An activity book allows kids to learn the history of Île de la Cité and have fun at the same time.

7, Parvis Notre-Dame-Place Jean-Paul-II, 2ᵉ.
+33 1 55 42 50 10.
Open Tues–Sun 10am–6pm.
Admission € 7, free for under-18s.
crypte.paris.fr

BEHIND THE SCENES OF THE PARIS METRO

Although you may take the metro every day, the Parisian underground railway network always saves a few surprises for you. Network operator RATP invites you to discover the ghost stations, ones that have fallen into disuse. Depending on the day and route, you can visit the control room for Line 1 or even watch a tunnel boring machine working on Line 12…
€5. Sign up at: tourisme93.com/ratp/

Cosmopolitan Paris:
travel the world without leaving the city

Beijing, Cairo, Moscow, Athens, New York… your dream destinations, but a little difficult when travelling with children. Why bother when all of these cultures are right here near you?

ASIA IN THE 13ᴱ

Paris's Chinatown is a neighbourhood in the thirteenth arrondissement, in the south-west of the city. Even a famous American fast food restaurant uses Chinese characters on its shop-front. Head for Boulevard Masséna to discover other unusual places that line the streets of this Paris district. Some of the Chinese and Vietnamese restaurants, such as Bambou, near Olympiades metro station, are absolute wonders. This place is ideal if you want to enjoy pho, skewers, noodles… all the typical Vietnamese dishes. The place has become a victim of its own success, so you'll have to wait a while if you haven't made a booking.

Paris 13ᵉ.

EGYPT IN THE 10ᴱ

A legendary cinema dating from 1920, **Louxor** closed down in 1983. However, a campaign by local residents of the Barbès neighbourhood and film buffs allowed it to be saved from ruin. After three years of restoration work and rebuilding, the cinema was reborn from the ashes. Films of all genres are shown here and a special place is given to creations from the countries of South America, Asia and Africa. Cultural events, film-making activities, film festivals and adult education film studies make it possible for everybody to appreciate this place.

170, Boulevard Magenta, 10ᵉ.
+33 1 44 63 96 96.
cinemalouxor.fr

CHINA IN THE 8ᴱ

Rising out of the Parisian mist like a red dragon, the pagoda-style architecture of **Maison Loo** contrasts with the classical elegance of the high-end eighth arrondissement. A sign shows that it belongs to a dealer in antiques. Since it was built in the 1920s, Maison Loo has housed the Oriental collections of a wealthy Chinese art dealer, Mr Loo. But the building itself is quite French. The work by the architect François Bloch was the result of the expatriate Loo's request to have a Chinese mansion in the heart of Paris that was large enough to accommodate all of his business.

48, Rue de Courcelles, 8ᵉ.
+33 1 45 61 06 93.

GREECE IN THE 9ᴱ

Did you know that there is Paris neighbourhood called 'New Athens'? In the ninth arrondissement, centred on the square, Place Saint-Georges, visitors are presented with private town houses in the Greek Revival style, built during the Romantic period. Although everything is worthy of admiration, particular attention should be given to house number 28 on the square. The Musée de la Vie Romantique is also found in this district, showcasing nineteenth-century European interior decoration.

RUSSIA IN THE 15ᴱ

A discreet Russian Orthodox church in the fifteenth arrondissement hides a surprising interior. Life in the church of Saint-Séraphin, consecrated in 1933, moves to the rhythm of divine liturgies, chanting workshops and catechesis. Upon entry, you realize that the church is completely made out of wood and that a tree is growing inside it.

91, Rue Lecourbe, 15ᵉ.

BRITTANY IN THE 15ᴱ

No, the Eiffel tower isn't the only beacon to guide aircraft and lost tourists into Paris. In 1996 a Breton lighthouse (yes, a real one) was transported from its native Brittany to live out its life happily in this Paris neighbourhood, connected to the Atlantic by its station. More than 10 metres tall and with the French and Breton flags fluttering in the breeze at its summit, it bears a sign on its rear, which can only be seen by travellers taking the train in the direction of Brittany, with the words: *Gloire aux marins-pêcheurs* (glory to sea-faring fishermen). The lighthouse is actually an advertisement for the former fishmonger, La Criée du Phare. And while you're in the neighbourhood, you should sample a traditional Breton galette or buckwheat crêpe at one of the many crêperies on Rue du Montparnasse.

69, Rue Castagnary, 15ᵉ.

NEW YORK IN PARIS

Just to recap, the Statue of Liberty is in New York. About that, everybody agrees. A gift from France in 1886, it was designed by Auguste Bartholdi and its metal structure was built by Gustave Eiffel.

But did you know that there are three replicas of different sizes in Paris? If you'd like to see them, you'll find one in the Luxembourg Gardens, another in front of the Musée des Arts et Métiers, and the most beautiful one on the Île aux Cygnes. Take your kids to look for them.

Jardin du Luxembourg, 6ᵉ.

Musée des Arts et Métiers, 3ᵉ.

Île aux Cygnes, 15ᵉ.

79

Paris from the air (or climb up to see Paris from above)

ARC DE TRIOMPHE
50 MÈTRES

TOP OF THE EIFFEL TOWER
301 MÈTRES

AIR DE PARIS HOT AIR
150 MÈTRES

80

MONTMARTRE
130 MÈTRES

BUTTES-CHAUMONT
VIEWPOINT
101 MÈTRES

DEPARTMENT STORE
ROOFTOP TERRACE

PARC DE BELLEVILLE
108 MÈTRES

TOP FLOOR OF THE
CENTRE POMPIDOU
46 MÈTRES

NOTRE-DAME
96 MÈTRES

PANTHÉON
83 MÈTRES

ROOFTOP AT
CITÉ DE LA MODE
ET DU DESIGN

TOUR
MONTPARNASSE
210 MÈTRES

Chapter 3
Dreaming, imagination and self-expression

Art lovers

Museum: visits and tours for the family

Little ones are also entitled to their share of culture, but museum visits aren't always much fun for the youngest kids. However, there are a number of outings that are suitable for children because they offer specific tours. For those with an obvious artistic leaning, or who are still developing one, here's an overview of the best cultural outings for kids.

CITY OF PARIS MUSEUMS

For a fun experience while visiting municipal museums, Paris Musées offers activity books on the permanent collections housed at the 14 museums operated by Paris city council. This allows kids to have fun while discovering the collections at Musée Carnavalet (history of Paris), Musée Cernuschi (Asian arts), the Petit Palais (fine art), MAM (modern art) and the Palais Galliera (fashion), to name a few.
€1 at the museum or for download at parismuseesjuniors.paris.fr

MUSÉE CARNAVALET

The oldest of the City of Paris museums covers the history of the French capital from its distant beginnings through to the present day. You can find a wide variety of exhibits: archaeological artefacts, views of Paris in the past, models of ancient monuments, iconic signs, historical scenes, portraits of famous Parisians… all of which explain the city's history to children through an audioguide with content designed especially for kids.

Another way for families to discover the museum is through storytelling sessions with a dramatic atmosphere.
16, Rue des Francs-Bourgeois, 3ᵉ.
+33 1 44 59 58 58.
Open Tues-Sun 10am-6pm. Free admission, audioguide €5. carnavalet.paris.fr

MAISON VICTOR HUGO

To give meaning to the texts kids will be reading at school, a visit to the poet's home in Place des Vosges is ideal.
The apartment Victor Hugo lived in between 1832 and 1848 reveals his life through three decisive periods in his life in the leading up to and after his exile on the island of Guernesey. The museum offers several themed visits with storytelling for children aged 6 and over, designed to present a subject based on either biographical events or on a literary text. The stories tell the life of the Hugo family, stories of dragons and monsters inspired by the the Chinese-style decoration of the apartment or based on the story of Notre-Dame or the character of Gavroche.
6, Place des Vosges, 4ᵉ. +33 1 42 72 10 16.
Open Tues-Sun 10am-6pm. Free admission, audioguide €5. maisonsvictorhugo.paris.fr

85

MUSEUM OF MODERN ART

Fauvism, Cubism, the School of Paris, abstract, New Realism, figurative and conceptual art forms… the art movements of the twentieth century are often difficult to understand for adults as they are for children. Fortunately, the City of Paris Museum of Modern Art creates activity books for the whole family to discover temporary exhibitions. Many different art workshops are also held for children aged 3–14.

11, Avenue du Président-Wilson, 16ᵉ.
+33 1 53 67 40 00.
Open Tues–Sun 10am–7pm.
Free admission. mam.paris.fr

MUSÉE D'ORSAY

There are hundreds of ways for children over 5 to discover Impressionism at the Musée d'Orsay on Wednesdays, at weekends and during school holidays. Practical art workshops, visits with a guest speaker or a young artist for 5–11-year-olds, lectures on current trends for teenagers, activity tours for families, free shows and concerts held every first Sunday of the month...

1, Rue de la Légion-d'Honneur, 7ᵉ.
Open every day, except Mon, 9am–6pm
(9am–9.15pm on Thur)
Activity tours for families: €4.50 per person.
musee-orsay.fr

MUSÉE DU LOUVRE

It is highly recommended that you visit this museum one part at a time. Your visit to the Louvre could take in one wing at a time, or one period at a time. Whether they prefer the Ancient Romans, Egyptians or Greeks or the great kings of France, your children's imaginations will run wild with inspiration by the works and objects from past times. You can hire a Nintendo DS to use as an interactive audioguide or down load a brochure for the themed 'Paris Mômes' (Paris Kids) tour. A large number of workshops and tours for children allow them to discover through games the drawings that Leonardo da Vinci and Delacroix made before they made the final artworks; an introduction to the hieroglyphic writing system, followed by deciphering an inscription; and how to make a fresco in the style of Botticelli or Fra Angelico, among others.

99, Rue de Rivoli, 1ᵉʳ. +33 1 40 20 53 17.
Open every day, except Tues, 9am–6pm.
Admission €12, free for under-18s,
audioguide €5.
louvre.fr

VISIT MUSEUMS IN YOUR OWN HOME

The City of Paris museums and the Musée d'Orsay offer virtual tours suited to children. These interactive sites allow you to explore the art in your own home in a fun way for kids.

parismuseesjuniors.paris.fr
musee-orsay.fr/une_minute/index.html

Budding artists

After contemplating works by the great artists, it's time to introduce your children to new cultural activities. Throughout the year, Paris is filled with workships to turn your kids into the artists of the future.

MUSÉE EN HERBE WORKSHOPS

Musée en Herbe is a museum devoted to children that offers loads of workshops for people of all ages and kids with different artistic preferences: stencil art, mail art, collage, T-shirt painting, clay modelling… Turn your little one into an artist of the future! Baby Z'Ateliers are workshops where children have fun by putting into practice what they were able to see in an exhibition, while P'tit Filou workshops use yoghurt pots to make works of art…
21, Rue Hérold, 1ᵉʳ.
+33 1 40 67 97 66.
Ateliers for children aged 2 years 6 months–12 years, €9–€16. musee-en-herbe.com

DECORATIVE ARTS

Ateliers du Carrousel give 122 different courses to more than 1,99 students every year. The 40 teachers, all professional artists offer year-long courses. Your artists in the making will be introduced to different practices and techniques: drawing, colour, charcoal, paint and collage, among others, in addition to clay modelling and comic workshops.
107, Rue de Rivoli, 1ᵉʳ. +33 1 44 55 57 50.
Workshops for 5–13-year-olds €160
for several days.
lesartsdecoratifs.fr

CITÉ DE L'ARCHITECTURE

On Wednesdays and Saturdays, and every day during school holidays, the Cité de l'Architecture welcomes children to its many workshops. Budding architects can choose to discover the art of construction from the Middle Ages to the present day, make frescoes and even design a mansion to satisfy the extravagant requests of an imaginary client.
1, Place du Trocadéro et du 11-Novembre, 16ᵉ.
+33 1 58 51 52 00.
Workshops for children over 7,
€8 for 90 minutes.
citechaillot.fr

87

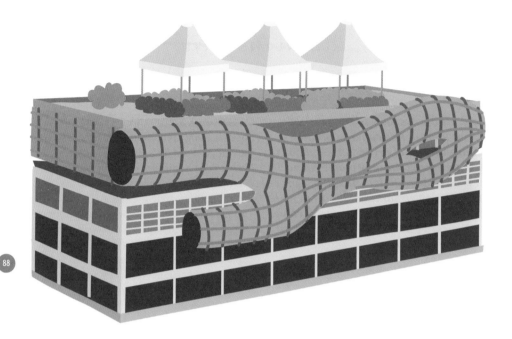

LITTLE MONETS

You're probably very familiar with Claude Monet's Water Lilies on display at the **Musée de l'Orangerie**, in the Tuileries Garden. But did you know that your children have the opportunity to surpass the master of Impressionism? They can reinterpret the painting in a two-hour-long workshop in the magnificent room where the painting is hung.

Jardin des Tuileries, 1ᵉʳ. +33 1 44 50 43 01.
Workshop for children aged 5–11.
musee-orangerie.fr

LE LITTLE PALAIS DE TOKYO

In order to make contemporary design more accessible to the youngest children, Le **Little Palais** is transformed alternately into a reading room, concert venue or art workshop. Accompanied by parents or a guide, children are taken on an extraordinary adventure into the world of contemporary art. 'Tok-Tok' workshops offer 5–7-year-olds and 8–10-year-olds discovery workshops as part of exhibitions.

13, Avenue du Président-Wilson, 16ᵉ.
+33 1 81 97 35 88.
Workshops for children aged 5–10 €6.
palaisdetokyo.com

QUAI BRANLY

The works on display at the **Musée du Quai Branly** are an endless source of wonder even for the youngest children because of the strange materials used to make and the fascinating stories told by objects. The museum offers a series of adventures to be shared by the whole family as they travel through time to discover the Maya, sorcerers of Africa and the native peoples of North America.

37, Quai Branly, 7ᵉ. +33 1 56 61 70 00.
Workshops for children aged 3–12 €8.
quaibranly.fr

Art in the open

You don't always have to rush through the corridors of museums to admire beautiful works of art in Paris. Indoor museums aren't the only places where art is on display. In fact, the streets of Paris offer a permanent exhibition, with statues decorating the cityscape. It comes as no surprise that the city is known as an 'open-air museum'.

STREET ART... ALL OVER THE EAST
A large number of wall paintings decorate the streets all over Belleville. And you just have to walk down the streets rue du Faubourg-du-Temple, rue Dénoyez, rue Jacques-Louvel-Tessier and rue Alibert to discover amazing works by lots of different street artists, both famous and unknown. You can find all the art described on the map created by paris-streetart.com.

THE STRAVINSKY FOUNTAIN A T THE CENTRE POMPIDOU
The Stravinsky Fountain was created in 1983 by Jean Tinguely and Niki de Saint Phalle. The sixteen sculptures pay tribute to the works of the composer Igor Stravinsky. All of them are mechanical, either black or coloured, and driven by water jets, giving free rein to children's imagination and dreams.
Rue Brise-Miche, 4ᵉ.

MUSÉE DE LA SCULPTURE EN PLEIN AIR
Located along Quai Saint-Bernard, between the bridges Pont de Sully Pont d'Austerlitz, **Musée de la Sculpture en Plein Air** is an open-air sculpture gallery to delight art lovers strolling along the Seine.
This garden and museum was designed by Daniel Badani and opened in Square Tino-Rossi in 1980. 30 works are spread out over a space of 2 hectares for everybody to admire, day or night. Works by great artists such as César Baldaccini, Constantin Brancusi, Alexander Archipenko, Ossip Zadkine, Émile Gilioli and Jean Arp stand next to others by less well-known artists.
Quai Saint-Bernard, 5ᵉ.

OSSIP ZADKINE, LA NAISSANCE DES FORMES
More recently, in the fourteenth arrondissement, an abstract work by Ossip Zadkine, La Naissance des Formes, can be admired near the museum devoted to this great twentieth-century sculptor. On his return from exile in the United States in 1947, Zadkine created a small piece in plaster with the name of *La Naissance des Formes*. Ten years later, he created this monumental version.
Allée Georges-Besse, on the corner of Bd Edgar-Quinet and Bd Raspail, 14ᵉ.

89

JOAN MIRÓ
AT SQUARE DE L'OISEAU-LUNAIRE

In the small garden of Square de l'Oiseau-Lunaire (formerly known as Square Blomet) in the fifteenth arrondissement, on the site of the workshops where many artists found success, pride of place is given to a statue by Joan Miró. Oiseau lunaire (Moon Bird) is a sculpture in bronze that the artist donated to the city of Paris in 1974.
Square de l'Oiseau-Lunaire, 15ᵉ.

FONTAINE DE L'OBSERVATOIRE

On Avenue de l'Observatoire, in the sixth arrondissement, one of the most impressive pieces of urban art can be found: the Fontaine de l'Observatoire. The upper section, representing the four parts of the world, was created by Jean-Baptiste Carpeaux and Pierre Legrain, while the dolphins are the work of Emmanuel Frémiet.
Avenue de l'Observatoire, 6ᵉ.

ARISTIDE MAILLOL

Between the Tuileries Garden and the Musée du Louvre, you can admire sixteen sculptures by Aristide Maillol, donated to the city of Paris in 1964 by Dina Vierny. One of the most famous sculptors of his time, Maillol brought about an artistic revolution and was a source of inspiration for many great artists, including Picasso, Brancusi and Matisse.
192, Rue de Rivoli, 1ᵉʳ.

LA BICYCLETTE ENSEVELIE

La Bicyclette Ensevelie (The Buried Bicycle) is a work by Claes Oldenburg and Coosje Van Bruggen installed in Parc de la Villette, between the lawns of the Prairie du Cercle Sud and the Prairie du Triangle. This monumental sculpture represents an assortment of bicycle parts (wheel, handlebar, pedal and seat) partly buried in the ground.
Parc de la Villette, 19ᵉ.

TRAM TOUR

Head off on an art-filled journey for the price of a metro ticket. Take the tram on the T3 line between Porte d'Aubervilliers and Porte de Vitry to explore a route filled with fifteen works by international artists. Using the interactive content on an iPad, a number of speakers show you how to see contemporary art and urban design in a new light.
€8, free for under-18s for a 2-hr tour.
Bookings on dedale.info

Not your typical museum

In Paris, every type of art has its home. The main art forms have their museums, and so do the more unusual types that kids find amusing. Let yourself be surprised by Paris's quirkier museums and share fun-filled times with the little ones.

STAR GAZING

Musée Grévin is one of the museums kids love the most. It offers you the chance to encounter leading historical figures and celebrities from our time. No fewer than 450 wax characters are represented there, and the impressive tour takes in the Hall of Mirrors, a cocktail bar and the history of France, among other things… Kids' favourites include Scrat from *Ice Age*, Tony Parker, Titeuf, Jenifer, Marsupilami, Mimi Mathy, Sébastien Loeb, Asterix and Mika. Themed visits with storytelling are available for children at weekends.
10, Boulevard Montmartre, 9ᵉ.
+33 1 47 70 83 97. / Open every day 10am–6pm.
Admission €23.50, €16.50 for online bookings
5 days in advance, free for children under 6.
Guided tours Sat and Sun, €20.50 per child.
grevin-paris.com

DOLLS' HOSPITAL

Musée de la Poupée takes you through two centuries of doll history. In their period settings, the dolls recreate periods in the past. Parents and grandparents will be able to find the sorts of dolls they had as children. Kids are also able to see how dolls are made, and also a doll hospital ready to treat dolls that are unwell.
28, Rue Beaubourg, 3ᵉ.
+33 1 42 72 73 11.

Open Tues–Sat 1–6pm.
Admission €8 for adults,
€4 for children aged 3–11.
museedelapoupeeparis.com

GOURMET HEAVEN

Warning; this place will make your mouth water! The Gourmet Chocolate Museum, also known as **Choco-Story**, brings to light 4,000 years of history, from the Olmec civilization to the present. You'll learn all there is to know about the history of cocoa beans, plus modern methods for manufacturing chocolate. Of course, you'll be able to taste different chocolate varieties made from beans from all over the world.
28, Boulevard de Bonne-Nouvelle, 10ᵉ.
+33 1 42 29 68 60. / Open every day 10am–6pm.
Admission €8, €6 for children aged 6–12,
free for children under 6.
museeduchocolat.fr

YOG'ART

Once a month, **Musée Guimet**, also known as Musée National des Arts Asiatiques, offers yoga classes for the family in the Lotus Room located on the same level as the museum gardens. These sessions allow parents and kids to do yoga and discover the museum collections in a fun and relaxing way. The classes are given by Ulrika Dezé, a yoga instructor who specializes in teaching children and families.
6, Place d'Iéna, 16ᵉ.
+33 1 56 52 53 45.
One Sat per month at 3pm.
€12 for adults,
€6.30 for children. guimet.fr

[We show you how]

A merry Christmas

Christmas is coming and the lights in the streets are there to remind you that the marathon is about to begin. You want to make this season a time for wonderful memories for your model children (who have been behaving themselves since posting the only letter they'll write all year)... So be quick, you're going to need all the ideas you can get! But the good thing is that Paris will help you to make the month of December a delight.

A CHRISTMAS SPECTACLE

One typically Parisian tradition is to admire department store Christmas window displays. Hordes of children crowd round these mini animated theatres, in keeping with a tradition that started in 1909, when the Bon Marché department store came up with the idea.

The star of these miniature spectacles is the work of the Dehix family, generations of puppeteers who pull the strings behind the scenes of this fantastical art at Galeries Lafayette and Printemps. If these magical moments captivate even the most indifferent among us, it's because they're the result of work that sometimes starts as early as February, and which involves model makers, decorators, carpenters, window dressers and electricians working around the puppeteer. An army of workers making sure the toy spectacle runs smoothly.

Bon Marché
24, Rue de Sèvres, 6ᵉ.
BHV Marais
52, Rue de Rivoli, 4ᵉ.
Galeries Lafayette
40-48, Boulevard Haussmann, 9ᵉ.
Le Printemps
64, Boulevard Haussmann, 9ᵉ.

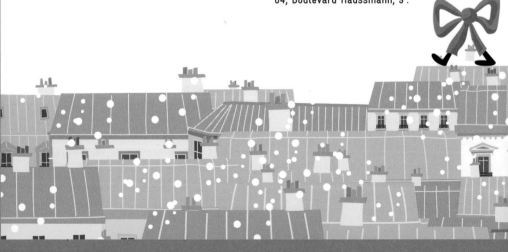

MERRY-GO-ROUND

After strolling down rue de Sèvres, Boulevard Haussmann and rue de Rivoli, you can admire the enormous Christmas tree in the square outside Notre-Dame and, if you like, the nativity scene inside the cathedral, and those in the Madeleine church or in the Sacré-Coeur. On the way, you'll most likely come across a merry-go-round, most of which are free during the Christmas and New Year holidays. Old-fashion merry-go-rounds are so beautiful, and it would be a shame not to get a closer look at them. The Musée des Arts Forains specializes in fairground attractions and houses a magnificent collection of old games, mechanical figures, music hall accessories and curios, avidly collected over 35 years by Jean-Paul Favart.

The museum holds the Festival du Merveilleux in the ten days after Christmas. There's no need to book at this time (unlike the rest of the year). There, the little ones are entertained by acrobats, jugglers and actors as they experience this magical place. The children leave the place with stars in their eyes.

Musée des Arts Forains Pavillons de Bercy 53, Avenue des Terroirs-de-France, 12ᵉ. +33 1 43 40 63 44. www.arts-forains.com

A list of all the free merry-go-rounds in Paris open to children from 20 Dec to 4 Jan, 10am–7pm can be found at www.parisinfo.co

[We show you how]

THE MOUNTAINS IN PARIS

Snow and ice begin to miraculously appear at Christmas time in certain parts of the city, where a 'mountain microclimate' brings joy to budding sports stars. You can take your kids to ride a luge or put on skis at Stade Charléty and Place Saint-Sulpice.

The square and surrounding streets hold a four-day event at the end of November known as Saint-Germain des Neiges, with little chalets, a snow garden for children and a ski jump for freestyle demonstrations. Don't worry; the ESF instructors land on a giant air mattress.

If after all these activities, you haven't won the prize for being the coolest parents in Paris, return the presents.

Charléty sur Neige Stade Charléty
99, Boulevard Kellermann, 13ᵉ.
24 Dec–4 Jan (except 1 Jan).
Open Mon–Sat 1.30–6.30pm (reception closes at 5pm).
Free admission.
Saint-Germain des Neiges
Place Saint-Sulpice, 6ᵉ.
4 days, late November. Free entertainment.
france-montagnes.com/saint-germain- des-neiges

A MAGICAL CHRISTMAS AT THE HÔTEL DE VILLE

The Hôtel de Ville, Paris's city hall, welcomes families to attend many Christmas workshops held in its concept store Paris Rendez-Vous. While the kids busy themselves in the world of Christmas, parents can do their Christmas shopping from the selection of very Parisian gifts to be found there. The icing on the cake, or on the yule log in this case, is that the entertainment is free.

29 Rue de Rivoli, 4ᵉ
Open Mon–Sat 10am–7pm
rendezvous.paris.fr

A RUSTIC CHRISTMAS MARKET

A few minutes from Paris, **Fermes de Gally** make the perfect setting for a country-style Christmas market, prettily illuminated by torchlight. Children will enjoy going back and forth between the animals, the Christmas trees and meeting Santa Claus, while eating waffles and roasted chestnuts. Leaving the kids do a workshop, where they listen to a Christmas story or make Christmas rolls, will give you a little respite.
Route de Bailly (D7), 78210 Saint-Cyr-l'École 01 30 14 60 60.
Open Mon–Sun 9.30am–7pm. Torchlight on Sat and Sun after 5pm.
ferme.gally.com

A NIGHT LIKE NO OTHER

Christmas time can also be an opportunity to have a special evening, spent going to the theatre, the circus, the ballet or the opera. Check out what's on in Paris in December well in advance. There are lots of shows that are just for kids. And why not plan for a wonderful New Year's Eve with them, instead of moping because you couldn't find a babysitter for that night. Dinner and show, magic show, cruise... Choose something to bring a sparkle to the eye and joy to the heart for the whole family.

Théâtre du Châtelet
1, Place du Châtelet, 1er.
+33 1 40 28 28 28.
chatelet-theatre.com

Le Double Fond
New Year's Eve dinner followed by magic show.
1, Place du Marché-Sainte-Catherine, 4e.
Bookings only on +33 1 42 71 40 20 or at resa@doublefond.com

Le Zèbre
Cabaret circus and dinner, followed by show.
63, Boulevard de Belleville, 11e.
Bookings only on +33 1 43 55 55 55.
lezebre.com

Let the music play

Singing

After watching The Voice *and* La Nouvelle Star *on TV and singing the latest Disney hit at the top of their lungs, have your kids got a taste for the taking the stage, mic in hand? There's no need to enter them into the next TV talent show – Paris opens its doors to their musical creativity.*

VOICE BEST

Your children aged 3½ and over can have individual or group lessons to make the most of their angelic voices. The lessons are given by teacher Leah Bicep, an artist who has backed Céline Dion and played one of the main roles in the musical *The Lion King*. At the end of the year, your little ones give a show that they will have been preparing on Wednesday or Saturday afternoons.

149, Rue de Rennes, 6ᵉ.
+33 6 72 84 71 97.
Group lessons for children aged 3–13 €400, 14–15 €450, 16 and over €500 for a full year.
Individual lessons for children aged 3–13 €450 for a full year,
children over 13 €270 a month.

MINI-STAR AND VOICE

Would you like your kids to have English lessons instead of singing songs? Here's the solution: **Kidjam** offers bilingual singing lessons for kids aged 7–9. With piano accompaniment, the teacher lets the children sing and introduces them to improvisation techniques. Lessons are given on Wednesday afternoons, with two sessions suited to the ages of your stars in the making.
See address on p. 70. kidjam.fr

LA CLEF ENCHANTÉE

If you're more into *Swan Lake* and *The Nutcracker* than rock or pop, La Clef Enchantée is an association that introduces children into the world of opera. From the age of 3, children in small groups study the history of music, piano, singing and music theory in a relaxed atmosphere.
5, Rue de Tracy, 2ᵉ.
+33 1 48 01 03 30.
laclefenchantee.org

MUSICALS

The **ENAC** Association in the fourteenth arrondissement offers a musical workshop that combines singing, music and movement for older kids (over 8s). Each session consists of warming up the body and voice, exercises and improvisation to gain awareness of the body in space, work on movements and texts, creation of characters, situations and interpersonal relations. Students select and interpret extracts from a wide variety of musicals and take part in putting on a show.
104, Rue du Château, 14ᵉ.
+33 1 40 56 95 53.
€459, reduced rate €339. enac.asso.fr

L'ÉCOLE DU MUSIC-HALL

This leading school specializing in children aged 6–15 introduces more developed kids to the art of variety entertainment. Using a musical repertoire ranging from France Gall to Jacques Dutronc, by way of *The Umbrellas of Cherbourg*, they learn to become dancers, singers and actors.
5, Passage des Taillandiers, 11ᵉ.
+33 1 77 32 81 47.
Young children aged 6+, older children aged 12+.
ecole.music.hall@gmail.com

LESSONS
COMMUNITY CENTRES
Whether classical, urban, modern, jazz, rock or styles from round the world, the 43 community centres operated by Paris city council offer a wide range of dance classes for young and old. In order to find what you want from this huge diversity, there's a very practical search engine on the quefaire.paris.fr website. It's up to you to make your choice.
quefaire.paris.fr/coursetlecons/

GIVE THEIR TRAINERS A WORKOUT
Do your kids never take off their *NYC* caps, draw graffiti all over their notebooks and play the latest rap hits over and over again? Then this dance school is just what the doctor ordered. **Juste Debout** specializes in hip-hop dance lessons for young children and teens. The place where they get to own their style while getting in some exercise.
3, Rue de l'Est, 20ᵉ.
+33 1 57 14 59 85. €15 per lesson.
juste-debout.com

PUT ON YOUR BALLET SLIPPERS
Ballerine&Calebasse offers early learning classes for children aged 4–5 to introduce them to dance. They are taught to experience the basics of the discipline, such as space, musicality, body awareness, the properties of movement and supporting the body with the feet. Then, when the children reach Year 2 at primary school, they can start classical dance lessons in a fantasy world of tutus and sequins, but the approach is demanding: control, flexibility and coordination are key.
30, Rue de Bruxelles, 9ᵉ. +33 6 88 77 07 61.
€330–360 per year. ballerineetcalebasse.com

PARTIES
GAÎTÉ-LYRIQUE
For the duration of exhibitions, **Gaîté-Lyrique** holds parties for children aged 5 and over, accompanied by their parents. Neofolk and electronic dance tunes adapted to children to give them a taste for music and the fun of the dance floor.
3 *bis*, Rue Papin, 3ᵉ. €5. gaite-lyrique.net

LE PETIT BAIN
Once a month, **Le Petit Bain Douche** is a real clubbing experience for kids aged 7–13 with everything they need to become stars on the dance floor. But don't worry; the sound levels are suited to sensitive ears and the bar only serves fruit juices and mocktails. Your only regret is that you can't get down on the floor and dance to the music played by the DJs under the spinning lights from the huge glitter ball. There's also a choreographer to give dance lessons and get the party moving.
7, Port de la Gare, 13ᵉ.
One Sun per month 3–5.30pm.
€8 for children (children over 13 not admitted).
petitbain.org

Playing and listening to music

Drums, electric guitar, violin, keyboards, bass…, whatever the instrument, it's always a pleasure for the ears when played well. You can pass on your love of good music, whether classical, rock, pop or another kind, to your children from a very young age. Here are five ideas to make this introduction a success and prevent the childhood traumas associated with the dreaded music theory class.

POUMPOUMTCHAK

This is a music school for children aged 4–16 that doesn't teach music theory. From the very first day, kids play real instruments and gradually learn guitar chords, basic drum rhythms, piano notes, the sound of the bass guitar and even singing techniques. A pop-rock song in French or English serves as a starting point for children to learn to play together and to record themselves in a studio, just like the pros. Teenagers can also put together their own rock group and work on songs of their choice, from a repertoire that includes The Beatles, Téléphone, The White Stripes, The Rolling Stones, Jacques Dutronc and -M-.
9, Rue Clapeyron, 8ᵉ. poumpoumtchak.com

LE CLUB POP

Here you won't find any boring music theory lessons, old-fashioned songs, or scales that make you weep. Music learning begins with a pop song by Michael Jackson or Jacques Dutronc. By breaking it down and identifying beats and chords, the children guess which instrument plays what. They can then try to reproduce the melodies on the drums, acoustic or electric guitar, keyboard or bass. When they're ready, the little musicians go into a studio and record their songs… it'll bring tears to a grandmother's eyes.
9, rue de Bellefond, 9ᵉ. +33 1 42 81 31 47. For children aged 3–10, €550 per year, €160 for courses during school holidays.
leclubpop.com

LES MARMOTS À GAVEAU

The famous **Salle Gaveau** in the eighth arrondissement offers educational workshops for children from the age of 3, which follow performances for young audiences. The early-learning music lessons for 3–5-year-olds are given by musicians trained to work with children, allowing kids to have their first experiences with music and develop their sense of creativity. Instruments, songs, nursery rhymes and games give these workshop their rhythm. For the over-5s, their mission is to form a small orchestra: keep up a tempo, play a different rhythm from that of their companions, learn the basics of rhythm… all of which will allow each child to learn what goes to making an orchestra.

45, Rue La Boétie, 8ᵉ. +33 1 49 53 05 07.
€20 for a workshop, €30 per person for show and workshop. sallegaveau.com

CITÉ DE LA MUSIQUE

Does your little one have an ear for music? Whether single sessions or a whole year, three or eight-session programmes, Cité de la Musique suits all tempos, from adagio to allegro. On offer are a wide variety of activities: early-learning music lessons for toddlers, introduction to instruments for 6–7-year-olds, percussion for everybody, family sessions… every musical preference is catered for.

221, Avenue Jean-Jaurès, 19ᵉ.
1 session: €10 for adults, €7 for children,
3 sessions:
€27 for adults, €19 for children, 8 sessions:
€65–85. Yearly: €160.

ROCK EN SEINE FESTIVAL

At the end of every summer, the Rock en Seine festival is held at the Domain National de Saint-Cloud. You're probably thinking that a festival isn't the place for parents to take their children. Well, you're wrong, because there's the Mini Rock en Seine, the first rock festival for 6–10-year-olds. From 4 p.m. until 10 p.m. there are a succession of costume workshops for budding rock stars, colouring workshops, readings of comics direct from the Angoulême festival, cooking workshops, dance sessions on a dance floor with strobe lighting for children, and storytelling to finish off the day on a more tranquil note.

Domaine National de Saint-Cloud.
End of August. rockenseine.com

On with the show

Circuses and more

If there's any activity where you can never guess what children's reactions will be, it's the circus. Some never get past the clowns, while others dream of climbing the trapeze or going into the cage with the lions. So, in order to introduce them to the art at their own pace, here are the best shows in the city and circus schools for those who can't wait to get started.

IN THE AUDIENCE
CIRQUE PINDER

Founded over 160 years ago, Cirque Pinder is an institution. High-flying trapeze artists, skilled jugglers, mischievous clowns, magicians and illusionists, tamers of white lions and other exotic animals, dancers on roller skates… Cirque Pinder knows how to surprise both young and old.
Pelouse de Reuilly, 12ᵉ.
Nov–Jan €7–50, depending on the seat position.
cirquepinder.com

CIRQUE D'HIVER

The Bouglione family have been making entertaining, thrilling and amazing children for more than 80 years. The Bougliones put on a great many spectacles at their Cirque d'Hiver venue: aerial dance, dogs, clowns, planes, the Chinese pole and especially the elephants and horses in an incredible and majestic display, followed by an acrobatic act featuring elephants.
110, Rue Amelot, 11ᵉ. +33 1 47 00 28 81.
Oct–Mar €27–50, depending on the seat position.
cirquedhiver.com

CIRQUE DU SOLEIL

When the sun is at its lowest point and the days are at their shortest, Cirque du Soleil put up their sets at Bercy. Every year a new story is told by the huge cast, and more than 15 million spectators marvel at the choreographies of these artists who travel the world. A North American show that has undeniably modernized the circus world.
Bercy Arena, 8, Boulevard de Bercy, 12ᵉ.
Dec €37–50, depending on the seat position.
cirquedusoleil.com

IN THE RING
MUNCIPAL COMMUNITY CENTRES

In most of Paris's arrondissements, municipal centres d'animations or community centres offer children aged 4–12 the chance to have a go at circus arts. Juggling, acrobatics, tightrope, trapeze and balancing… all are techniques that allow children to become aware of their bodies, express their creativity and improve their motor skills and dexterity. **Addresses available on quefaire.paris.fr/all/ cirque**

CIRQUE ÉLECTRIQUE

The Cirque Électrique school offers an introduction to the practical side of the art, from acting to taking risks. Workshops for adults and children take place all year round and are divided into different programmes, resulting in the creation and staging of shows. Under the school's big top, children aged 4–14 come every week to take part in programmes that teach acrobatics and aerial and balancing moves to express their passion for the circus.
Place du Maquis-du-Vercors, 18ᵉ.
+33 9 54 54 47 24.
cirque-electrique.com

The theatre: in the audience and on the stage

Dancing, singing, doing a circus act... whatever they're into, getting up on the stage gives children confidence in their everyday life. Of all the learning experiences, theatre is without a doubt the best way to work on children's natural shyness and stimulate their creativity.

IN THE AUDIENCE
CITY OF PARIS THEATRES
The Théâtre de la Ville, Théâtre des Abbesses and six associated theatres offer a programme suitable for kids.
Once they turn 5, they can attend theatre, dance, music and art shows. The great classics, such as Donkey-Skin, Beauty and the Beast and works by the Brothers Grimm are put on for them.
theatredelaville-paris.com

COMÉDIE-FRANÇAISE
A number of plays on the Comédie-Française programme are suitable for young audiences over the age of 10. This provides children with the best possible conditions in which to discover the great classics of the theatre, such as Molière, Labiche, Anouilh and Feydeu.
1, Place Colette, 1ᵉʳ.
+33 825 10 16 80.
comedie-francaise.fr

THÉÂTRE ASTRAL
Located inside Paris's Parc Floral, the Théâtre Astral presents a selection of plays throughout the year that are especially for children, mostly aged 3 and over. In addition to its own company's performances, the theatre regularly hosts performances by other companies in order to offer children the widest selection.
Parc Floral, Bois de Vincennes, 12ᵉ.
+33 1 49 72 79 06. €7.50.
theatreastral.com

THÉÂTRE DU GYMNASE MARIE-BELL
This famous theatre in the Grands Boulevards neighbourhood stages educational shows that offer kids aged 6 and over an entertaining way to learn English. Certain parts of the play are in English to provide the children with vocabulary.
38, Boulevard de Bonne-Nouvelle, 10ᵉ.
+33 1 42 46 79 79.
theatredugymnase.com

CHRISTMAS OUTING
As the Christmas holidays approach, many theatres present plays and shows for toddlers. The shows are inspired by fairy tales by Perrault or the Brothers Grimm, popular comics and great French poets throughout history. You are advised to check out the Théâtre Saint-Georges, Comédie Bastille, Théâtre le Ranelagh (Le Petit Ranelagh), Comédie de Paris, Espace Pierre-Cardin and even the Folies Bergère to find the perfect show for your kids.

106

ON THE STAGE
THÉÂTRE DE CLÉMENTINE

For children aged 5–17, this theatre offers courses in small groups, divided by ages, to develop their imagination, control their emotions and master the art of speaking. Children interpret a number of roles in plays and from literary texts, poems and fairy tales, and work on their voice, singing, gestures and the traits of different characters.

73, Rue des Cévennes, 15ᵉ. +33 6 60 85 55 94. €150 / 3-month term. letheatredeclementine.fr

THÉÂTRE PANDORA

In groups of 12 children, **Compagnie Maya** offers early-learning theatre courses for 3-4-year-olds and workshops for 5–15-year-olds that enable them to develop their imaginations and skill in repartee while encouraging them to speak in public and listen to their partners. But above all, the verbal ping pong that children play is good-natured and allows their personalities to contribute to an end-of-year performance.

30, Rue Keller, 11ᵉ. +33 6 12 96 65 98. €385-415 / year. compagniemaya.com

FOLIE THÉÂTRE

By means of games and theatre exercises, games and educational activities, children are introduced to the art of theatre. For the first half of the year, the exercises focus on controlling the body, voice, concentration and improvisation, among other things. Older kids also work on texts and the construction of characters. For them, the second half of the year is devoted to the staging of an end-of-year performance.

6, Rue de la Folie-Méricourt, 11ᵉ. +33 1 43 55 14 80. €155 / 3-month term. folietheatre.com

MUNICIPAL COMMUNITY CENTRES

Municipal community centres offer courses for children. Body expression, theatre games (diction, breathing, listening and group work) and improvisation form part of the programme.

Addresses available on quefaire.paris.fr/all/théâtre

Puppet shows

The parks and gardens of Paris offer a wide range of children's shows, such as concerts, storytelling and puppet theatres. Puppet theatres are ideal for familiarizing children with watching shows.

PUPPET THEATRE AT PARC MONTSOURIS

The marionette shows at Parc Montsouris date back to 1930 and are housed in a small theatre with a cozy atmosphere. The floral decoration, smell, old trumpets, small club chairs for children and comfortable folding chairs for parents give this listed building its unique character.
Avenue Reille-Rue Gazan, 14ᵉ. +33 6 07 77 85 42.
Shows Wed 3pm and 4pm, Sat, Sun and school holidays 11am–5pm.
€4 children aged 1–8.
guignol-parcmontsouris.com

THÉÂTRE DE MARIONNETTES

Located on the edge of the Bois de Vincennes in Saint-Mandé, this theatres brings marionettes to life: the Mice dance; the Fox converses with the Hen; Little Red Riding Hood is a clown; the Marchioness leads the ball.
Orée du Bois de Vincennes, 12ᵉ.
+33 6 75 23 45 89.
Shows Wed, Sat and Sun 3.30pm and 4.30pm.
€3.50 children aged 3 and over.
guignol-parcmontsouris.com

THÉÂTRE DE GUIGNOL DES CHAMPS-ÉLYSÉES

On the Champs-Élysées, Théâtre de Guignol, also known as Le Vraie Guignolet, comes to life and children take part in an outrageously funny show.
Cnr Avenue Matignon and Avenue Gabriel, 8ᵉ.
+33 1 42 45 38 30.
Shows Wed, Sat, Sun and school holidays 3pm, 4pm and 5pm.
€4 children aged 3 and over. theatreguignol.fr

THÉÂTRE DE GUIGNOL AT PARC FLORAL

Guignol has been the star of the puppet shows here since 1808, and many children continue to laugh and urge him on through his adventures. He sets out to encounter the natives of America, wild animals in Africa, dragons in Asia and even a witch in the Bois de Vincennes.
Main entrance to Parc Floral, 12ᵉ.
Shows Wed, Sat, Sun and school holidays. 3pm and 4pm.
€2.80 children aged 2½ and over.
guignolparcfloral.com

LE GUIGNOL DE PARIS AT PARC DES BUTTES-CHAUMONT

Le Guignol de Paris is located at the top of Parc des Buttes-Chaumont, in the nineteenth arrondissement. This puppet theatre presents adaptations of fairy tales and popular novels, along with the traditional Lyonnais repertoire, bringing fantasy and fun to young and old alike.

Entrance at the cnr Avenue Simon-Bolivar and Rue Botzaris, 19ᵉ.

+33 6 98 99 66 24.

Shows Wed, Sat, Sun and school holidays 3pm, 4pm and 5pm.

€4 children aged 1–8.

guignol-butteschaumont.com

THÉÂTRE GUIGNOL ANATOLE

This puppet theatre has been in Parc des Buttes-Chaumont since 1892 and presents updated Guignol shows drawn from both the Lyonnais and Parisian traditions.

This is one of the last open-air puppet theatres in Paris, which gives it a special charm.

Entrace opposite the mairie (town hall) of the 19ᵉ arrondissement

+33 1 40 30 97 60.

Shows Apr–mid-Oct.

€4 children aged 2 and over.

guignol-paris.com

PUPPET THEATRE AT THE JARDIN D'ACCLIMATATION

Lovers of Guignol shows are invited to the large, beautiful and comfortable marionette theatre with capacity for 200 people housed in the great stables built by Napoleon III in the Jardin d'Acclimatation.

Bois de Boulogne, 16ᵉ.

+33 7 60 25 77 33.

Shows Wed, Sat, Sun and school holidays. 3pm and 4pm.

children over 2 Free admission with garden entry ticket.

jardindacclimatation.fr/activite/theatre-de-guignol/

THÉÂTRE DE MARIONNETTES DU PARC GEORGES-BRASSENS

Built in 1987, this theatre presents shows featuring the character of Polchinelle (Pulcinella), much loved by children.

1287, Rue Cortot, 15ᵉ.

+33 1 48 42 51 80.

Shows Wed, Sat, Sun and school holidays 4pm and 6pm.

€4 children aged 2 and over.

marionnettes-parc-brassens.fr

DESIGN YOUR OWN PUPPETS AT MUSÉE GUIMET

Musée Guimet invites children aged 7 and over to learn about Cambodia and Indonesia by making puppets.

They are taught to bring four great heroes to life: a brave prince exiled in a forest; his wife; his faithful companion, the head of an army of monkeys; and a terrible demon who threatens the other characters. Four characters and four puppets to make that lead you into the epic world of the Ramayana (one of the two greatest stories of India) and the living traditions of South-East Asia.

6, Place d'Iéna, 16ᵉ. Bookings only.

+33 1 56 52 53 45.

guimet.fr

The magician's apprentice

Abracadabra! This word is a little difficult for your little ones to pronounce at first, but once mastered it will be used at every possible chance. Even the cat will be subjected to sleight of hand… so make sure your kids' magic tricks are successful and let them have fun with them.

MUSÉE DE LA MAGIE

Is your child obsessed with magic? Musée de la Magie showcases the wonderful world of magicians and conjurers from the eighteenth century to the present day. Let them enter into the world of illusion guided by a magician, and finish the tour with a magic show. A gallery of optical illusions, distorting mirrors and magic shop are also part of the programme.
11, Rue Saint-Paul, 4ᵉ. +33 1 42 72 13 26.
Shows Wed, Sat and Sun 2–7pm. Admission €9, €7 for children aged 3–12.
museedelamagie.com

MUNCIPAL COMMUNITY CENTRES

Paris's municipal community centres offer magic lessons for all ages and all levels. Children can learn small tricks and present them in a magic show at the end of the course. Because they enter into the very secret world of magicians, they aren't likely to reveal what lies behind their tricks.
Addresses available on quefaire.paris.fr/all/magie

CERCLE FRANÇAIS DE L'ILLUSION

After three conjuring lessons, children can master the secret techniques for doing magic tricks, taught to them by genuine illusionists. Three advanced courses are also offered so they can take their magic even further.
4, Rue Titon, 11ᵉ.
€50 for 3 hrs introductory lessons.
illusionniste.org

BIRTHDAY MAGIC

If you're thinking about adding a touch of extravagance and surprise to a child's birthday party, you can have a magician come to your home to perform a show lasting one or two hours. Kids are fascinated by tricks, and the appearance of tame dove or angora rabbit that they can pet will amaze them.
And as a bonus, the magician is also a balloon modeller who can make children's dreams a reality on request.
Dream Night.
+33 1 69 01 69 69.
dream-night.fr

OUTFITTING A MAGICIAN

The mecca for magicians is found not far from Paris, in Châtillon. There you can find more than 10,000 accessories, including magic rings, 'special' decks of cards, illusionists' scarves and canes.
8 *bis*, Rue de Malakoff, 92320 Châtillon.
+33 1 71 17 75 45.
paris-magic.com

Film buffs

With more than 150 independent cinema screens, Paris remains the undisputed capital for film buffs. There's sure to be something to suit, regardless of taste, age or neighbourhood. Many of the city's cinemas cater for children, which is something to keep in mind for a Wednesday afternoon or rainy school holidays.

STUDIO DES URSULINES

Opened in 2003, this is where you can encounter 3-year-olds who are here to see *Panda! Go, Panda!* or teenagers attending a screening of *Taxi Driver* with the film club for secondary-school students. This cinema can inspire career choices, given that certain people who came to see a film for the first time while in their pre-school years are now studying at a film school.

When you think about it, it seems that there's actually little distinction between a young audience and an adult audience, given that Charlie Chaplin can make a 5-year-old laugh and a 77-year-old film enthusiast can appreciate a Studio Ghibli production.
10, Rue des Ursulines, 5ᵉ. +33 1 56 81 15 20.
€8.20, €4 for children under 14.
studiodesursulines.com

FORUM DES IMAGES

Children aged between 18 months and 11 years are considered film buffs in their own right at the Forum des Images. On Wednesdays and Saturdays, afternoon sessions are held consisting of a film screening, a debate and snacks. It gives you the opportunity to (re)discover classics, animated films, cartoons, comedies, preview showings, films with live musical accompaniment of all kinds and for all ages on the big screen.

The Salle des Collections, an on-demand screening room, offers 150 films for children aged 3–12. Cartoons and full-length feature films are classified by age and subject, including: *Le Petit Mécano, The Triplets of Belleville, The Young Girls of Rochefort* and *Zazie dans le métro.* There are also cinema games for you to test your kids' knowledge or allow them to control the images, editing and sound.
2, Rue du Cinéma, 1ᵉʳ. +33 1 44 76 63 00.
forumdesimages.fr

MK2 BOUT'CHOU

A child's first time at the cinema can be an uphill battle for parents. So, to get off on the right foot, MK2 cinemas had the bright idea of holding toddlers' cinema sessions for children from the age of 3. The sound is easy on the ears; the films last less than an hour; and the lighting is subdued.
Cinémas MK2 Quai de Loire, Nation and Bibliothèque.
Wed, Sat and Sun, starting at 9.50am.
Admission €4 per person.

MK2 JUNIOR

From the age of 5, MK2 cinemas also have something to suit budding film buffs with different series of programmed screenings. Screenings take place on Wednesdays, Saturdays and Sundays at the three Paris cinemas. Take advantage to discover the superb cinema inside the Grand Palais. Highly recommended.

Cinémas MK2 Quai de Seine,
Gambetta and Grand Palais.
Wed, Sat and Sun, starting at 9.50am.
Admission €4 per person.

LA GÉODE

This giant hemispherical screen in Parc de la Villette plunges filmgoers deep into the image. They show documentaries on dolphins, coral reefs, India and special effects.

26, Avenue Corentin-Cariou, 19ᵉ.
+33 1 40 05 79 99.
€10.50.
lageode.fr

CHAPLIN DENFERT

This cinema has three small auditoriums that screen a host of animated films and recently released films for children on Wednesdays and at weekends. You can also celebrate your children's birthday parties there with all their friends. Besides the popcorn and sweets, the cinema also provides a workshop of your choice.

24, Place Denfert-Rochereau, 14ᵉ.
+33 1 43 21 41 01.
cinemadenfert.fr

GRAND REX

The largest cinema in Europe shows you what goes on behind the scenes. Listed as a historic monument, this giant cinema can hold as many as 2,800 people. Its remarkable interior decoration and architecture make it one of the last sanctuaries of film.

A 40-minute tour takes in the space behind the big screen, behind the scenes and to the projection room and other technical spaces.

1, Boulevard Poissonnière, 2ᵉ.
+33 1 45 08 93 89.
Open Wed–Sun 10am–5pm.
Admission €10 for adults, €6.50 for under-18s.
legrandrex.com

ART LUDIQUE

This museum is a mecca for young and old alike who are lovers of comics, manga, video games, cinema and animated films.

Art Ludique's purely temporary exhibitions showcase the designers of a world that has shaped our imagination. Kids become immersed in the drawings, paintings and sculptures made by the large animation studios, and the graphic design behind superheroes, sets, films and comic characters. They are shown what goes on behind the scenes in the world of graphic design.

Cité de la Mode & du Design, 34, Quai d'Austerlitz, 13ᵉ.
+33 1 45 70 09 49.
Open every day except Tues, 10am–8pm.
Admission €15.50, €10 for children aged 4–12.
artludique.com

[We show you how]
Winter fun

The holidays have arrived and winter is dragging on. The kids show obvious signs of fatigue, as do their parents. Paris provides opportunities to let off steam so that you don't turn as dull as the weather.

FESTIVE MADNESS: CARNIVAL

We may be unaware of it, but carnival has been celebrated in Paris since the dawn of time. Although the streets were quiet for about 50 years, it was restored to its rightful place in 1998 through the Droite à la Culture association. It's a wonderful occasion for the family to join the parade every year. And because it's a time for complete freedom, children love carnival. The parade has a theme, but it's up to you whether you follow it or not.

Promenade du Bœuf Gras (carnival parade) route: around Place Gambetta and then to Place de la République.
carnaval-paris.org

When it comes to the matter of a costume, for some more creative parents a piece of felt and a couple of snips with the scissors is enough to make an outfit their child has always dreamed of; others find specialist shops in Paris where they can stock up on red noses, psychedelic wigs, superhero capes and princess tiaras.

Au Clown de la République
11, Boulevard Saint-Martin, 3ᵉ.
+33 1 42 72 73 73.
Open Tues-Sat 10am-7pm, Mon 11am-7pm.
marais.evous.fr/Au-Clown-de-la-Republique

La Joie pour Tous
37, Boulevard Saint-Germain, 5ᵉ.
+33 1 43 54 98 67.
Open Tues-Sat 10am-1pm and 2.45-7.30pm.
lajoiepourtous-fete.com

Aux Feux de la Fête
135 bis, Bd du Montparnasse, 6ᵉ.
+33 1 43 20 60 00.
Open Tues-Fri 10am-1pm and 2-7.30pm
Sat 10am-7pm.
auxfeuxdelafete.com

Au Fou Rire
22 bis, Rue du Faubourg-Montmartre, 9ᵉ.
+33 1 48 24 75 82.
Open Mon-Sat 9.30am-7.30pm.
aufourire.com

Clown Montmartre
22, Rue du Faubourg-Montmartre, 9ᵉ.
+33 1 47 70 05 93
Open Mon-Sat 9.30am-7pm.
clown.fr

114

Au Cotillon Moderne
13, Boulevard Voltaire, 11ᵉ. +33 1 47 00 43 93.
Open Mon–Sat 9.30am–7pm.
cotillonmoderne.fr

Académie du Bal Costumé
22, Avenue Ledru-Rollin, 12ᵉ. +33 1 43 47 06 08.
Open Mon–Sat 10am–7pm.
evous.fr/Academie-du-Bal-Costume,1120031.html

MARDI GRAS, T'EN VA PAS, J'FERAI DES CRÊPES ET T'EN AURAS

If there's one recipe to keep handy when you have children, it's crêpes (pancakes), the typical thing to have on Mardi Gras (Shrove Tuesday). You should make a pile of them because crêpes keep very well in the fridge wrapped in aluminium foil. In fact, your little ones aren't all that fussy, and 3-year-olds will gladly help out with the batter. The objects of their desire are very quick to make. The only thing left to do is cook them and flip them over.

To make a dozen crêpes:
200 g (12 tbsp) flour 4 eggs
500 ml semi-skimmed milk
200 ml sparkling water
Mix the ingredients together in a mixer and leave to stand for one hour. The sparkling water will make the batter fluffier.
For the filling, as an alternative to the famous spread, suggest honey, jam, maple syrup or icing sugar drizzled with a little lemon juice. You can also melt a knob of butter over the crêpe and sprinkle with cocoa powder for a real treat.

SKATING TO MUSIC

Ice skating to music is an affordable pleasure in Paris. Protected from the weather, you can watch your kids progress at one of the two skating rinks that are open all year. The one at the Palais Omnisports de Paris-Bercy was given a facelift in 2014 and has a surface area of 1,500 square metres. There is a festive atmosphere for 'breaking the ice' at the Pailleron rink, with a surface of 800 square metres, which also has a time slot reserved for families on Sunday mornings and every morning during the school holidays.
A team of six qualified youth workers and instructors ensure totally safe skating (children up to the age of 10 are to be accompanied by their parents).

Espace Glace Pailleron
32, Rue Édouard-Pailleron, 19ᵉ.
+33 1 47 20 27 70.
Open every day (opening hours on their website).
Family skating: Sun and every day during school holidays 10am–12 noon.
pailleron19.com

Patinoire Sonja Henie - Palais Omnisports de Paris-Bercy
Boulevard de Bercy, 12ᵉ. +33 1 40 02 60 60.
Opening hours at: bercy.fr/patinoire

And for the ice-obsessed, **Club des Français Volants** ice hockey club offers quality year-round training to all hockey players and skaters, young and old.
francais-volants.org

Chapter 4
Meals, snacks and treats

Yummy!

Ice-cream parlours

¡Qué calor! As it finally emerges from its hiding place, the sun awakens in us the urge for something cold. Here's a small selection of the best ice-cream parlours in Paris to appease your longings and indulge kids' taste buds with a frozen treat.

BERTHILLON

Still trading after half a century, Berthillon is one of the oldest ice-cream parlours in the city. In fact, it's considered one of the ten best ice-cream parlours in the world.

No preservatives, sweeteners or acidifiers are used here, only natural ingredients. Their ice cream is made from milk, cream and eggs, while their flavourings are made from cocoa and vanilla. A must for the gourmets that we are. Their speciality: wild strawberry sorbet – absolutely incredible.

31, Rue Saint-Louis-en-l'Île, 4ᵉ.
+33 1 43 54 31 61.
Open Wed–Sun 10am–8pm.
berthillon.fr

POZZETTO

For a short break to cool down in the Marais, nothing beats an ice cream at Pozzetto. Named after the bain-marie system used by master Italian gelato-makers, Pozzetto prefers to pleasure the palate over the eye. They limit themselves to 12 flavours so that they can be made daily from fresh ingredients, a guarantee of quality. In keeping with the Italian tradition, they use a spatula rather than a scoop to serve the ice cream. The best one? Pistachio.

39, rue du Roi-de-Sicile, 4ᵉ. +33 1 42 77 08 64.
Open every day 12 noon–12 midnight.
pozzetto.biz

GELATI D'ALBERTO

People come to Gelati d'Alberto to treat themselves to artisan ice cream, but especially to see the skill and creativity involved in making their ice-cream flowers. Because the special thing about these ice creams is that they're shaped like rose petals. Choose from among the 36 flavours and you'll be presented with a multi-coloured open rose. What could be more romantic for a little princess? By the way, the milk they use is organic, and the Chantilly cream is home-made. A guaranteed burst of flavour and creaminess.

45, Rue Mouffetard, 5ᵉ.
12, Rue des Lombards, 4ᵉ. +33 1 77 11 44 55.
Open every day 12 noon–12 midnight.
gelatidalberto.com

AMORINO

For many, Amorino is THE best ice cream parlour, whether in France or in Italy. Founded in 2002 by two childhood friends, Cristiano Sereni and Paolo Benassi, Amorino seem to know how to combine all the ingredients for success. Quality, naturalness and variety are the key. Here too, the ice creams are sculpted into flowers. And the cherry on the cake? You can order as many flavours as you want as long as they fit in the cup.

20 shops in Paris. amorino.com

MARGUERITE DU PRÉ

The products used by Marguerite du Pré come directly from the farm. Their food truck decorated with a cool gingham print drives round Paris to offer 100 per cent organic frozen yoghurt that is made in France. 100 per cent natural, fat-free, gluten-free and free of artificial colourings and preservatives, it's a pleasure that should be taken without moderation.

Factory & Co
23, Cour Saint-Émilion, 12ᵉ.
Open every day 12 noon–11pm.
margueritedupre.fr

GLAZED

Are you fed up with the conventional vanilla and chocolate? Glazed aims to provoke by inventing flavours you could never have imagined: Smoke on the Water, Black Sugar Sex Magic, Orange Mécanique (clockwork orange). As a bonus, there's a subscription system that allows you to pay for three months' worth of ice cream, delivered directly to your home!

54, Rue des Martyrs, 9ᵉ. +33 9 81 62 47 09.
Open Mon–Thurs 12.30–8pm, Fri 12.30–10pm,
Sat 10am–10pm, Sun 10am–7.30pm.
contact@glaces-glazed.com

PIERRE HERMÉ

Refined ice cream, just like the flavours it comes in. There are also novelties to discover, such Satine, a frozen cheesecake, or ice cream with macaroons – amazing! Pierre Hermé likes contrasts and puts together flavours without letting them mix, which is an art form in itself.

11 shops in Paris.
pierreherme.com

RAIMO

If you want to be spoilt for choice when it comes to ice cream and sorbet, go to this 65-year-old ice-cream parlour. According to some, they're even better than the scoops served at Berthillon. But you can be the judge of that.

63, Boulevard de Reuilly, 12ᵉ.
+33 1 43 43 70 17.
Open Mon–Sun
10.30am–10.30pm.
raimo.fr

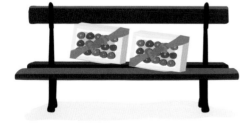

The best confectioners in Paris

If you want to treat your palate without telling your dentist, here are the sweetest addresses. Confectionery, chocolates, cakes… you're sure to find whatever you fancy. It's good to indulge the family.

À LA MÈRE DE FAMILLE
Entering through the doors or À la Mère de Famille is like going into a museum of French confectionery. This timeless, magical shop takes us back in time to our parents and grandparents' childhood. The place is decorated with mouth-watering sweets, nougat, *calissons*, marzipan fruits, chocolates and bonbons.
35, Rue du Faubourg-Montmartre, 9e.
+33 1 47 70 83 69.
Open Mon–Sat 9.30am–8pm, Sun 10am–1pm.
lameredefamille.com

KÄRAMELL
A little less authentic, but just as delicious are Käramell's Scandinavian sweets. Jars of sweets, 'Merlin's pills' and other surprises await one thing: to satisfy your sweet tooth.
15, Rue des Martyrs, 9e.
+33 1 53 21 91 77.
Open Tues–Sat 11am–8pm, Sun 10am–7pm.
karamell.fr

LE BONBON AU PALAIS
In a classroom straight out of a 1950s film, George invites you on a colourful journey back to childhood among his jars filled with confectionery and bonbons brought in from the four corners of France. Old-fashioned sweets, candied fruit, pâtes de fruits, calissons and chocolates… a taste of the best in French confectionery.
19, Rue Monge, 5e. +33 1 78 56 15 72.
Open Tues–Sat 10.30am–7.30pm.
bonbonsaupalais.fr

121

LA MAISON DES BONBONS
Entering this tiny shop in Rue Mouton-Duvernet will bring a twinkle to your eye. The senses are assailed by colours everywhere, and especially by sweets of all sorts. Feast your eyes on the *roudoudou* shell-shaped sweets, salted butter caramels, canes in barley sugar and marshmallows, and on the vintage tins with their quirky humour, assorted objects, flowery tableware, soft toys… magic and humour have a special place here.
14, Rue Mouton-Duvernet, 14e.
Open Tues–Sat 11am–7.30pm.
+ 33 1 45 41 35 55.

CONFISERIE RIVOLI

A little like À la Mère de Famille, Confiserie Rivoli has kept its old-world charm. You just have to look into the shop window with its huge marshmallow lollipops to make your mouth water. This confectionery wholesaler, which also sells to the public, also offers old-fashioned sweets, sugared almonds, original artisan confectionery, Belgian chocolates and *marrons glacés in season, pâtes de fruits, jellies, lollipops, multi-coloured marshmallows, liquorice, honey, biscuits and regional specialities, among others.*
17, Rue de Rivoli, 4ᵉ.
+33 1 42 72 80 90.
Open Mon 2–6.45pm, Tues–Sat 10am–6.45pm.

LA CURE GOURMANDE

Do you know the tale of Hansel and Gretel? La Cure Gourmande will immediately transport you there. Although it isn't made of gingerbread, this shop is piled floor to ceiling with sweet treats. There's something for everybody, whether you're a lover of soft caramels, bonbons, chocolate or cakes.
6 shops in Paris.
la-cure-gourmande.fr

Children welcome

News for parents who are dying to go out: Eating at a restaurant or going out for a drink isn't always easy when you have to take your children. The little ones get bored in an adults' world; they don't find the food to their taste; and you have to neglect your friends while you attend to them. There are cafés and restaurants in Paris that welcome parents with their children, providing an opportunity to combine pleasure and fun.

CAFÉZOÏDE

In this grand bazaar, kids reign supreme. The rules of this culture café are simple: admission is for children from newborns through to the age of 16 accompanied by a responsible adult. There are many activities available and the guiding principle is to give creativity a free reign.

Theatre, art, computer and musical activities are provided for them.

92 *bis*, Quai de la Loire, 19ᵉ.

+33 1 42 38 26 37.

Open Wed–Sun 10am–6pm.

cafezoide.asso.fr

HOME SWEET MÔMES

This is the first café for parents and children in the Goutte d'Or neighbourhood. It's for children under the age of 16 and allows them to share fun moments with their families through a variety of activity workshops, including a film club, painting, cooking, gardening, dance, and so on. An affordable lunch is available.

1, Rue Fleury, 18ᵉ. Open Sun 11am–6pm.
homesweetmomes.com

LES 400 COUPS

This leading restaurant for parents AND children offers good home-style, seasonal cuisine. Located a stone's throw away from Parc des Buttes-Chaumont, this little haven of tranquillity suitable for even the littlest ones offers children's, brunch and snack set menus. While mum and dad have lunch, they play, make friends and make use of a kitchenette to prepare their own 'meal'. On the practical side, everything is provided: play space, deck chairs, high chairs, play mats, childcare equipment… In other words, it's a parent's paradise!

12 *bis*, Rue de la Villette, 19ᵉ.
+33 1 40 40 77 78.
Open Wed 11.30am–3pm, Thurs and Fri 12 noon–3pm and 7–10pm, Sat 10.30am–10pm, Sun 10.30am–6pm.
les400coups.eu

L'OYA CAFÉ

It's playtime, kids! Head for L'Oya Café at teatime for a fun game of cards or board games. With more than 500 games, you'll be spoilt for choice, and you can spend the whole evening there.

25, Rue de la Reine-Blanche, 13ᵉ.
+33 1 47 07 59 59.
Open Tues–Sat 2pm–12 midnight, Sun 2–9pm.
oya.fr

UN AIR DE FAMILLE

Located in the middle of six neighbourhood schools, this place welcomes children aged 3–10 at teatime with lots of home-made goodies. When parents arrive, they can either have something to eat or take a yoga or Pilates class, or a shiatsu or sophrology session, while the kids are kept busy with cultural or sports workshops.

26, Rue du Château-Landon, 10ᵉ.
+33 1 42 05 01 24.
Open Mon–Fri 9am–8pm, Sat 10am–12 noon.
air-de-famille.fr

LA MAISON VÉLIB'EXKI

An urban oasis for Parisian fans of cycling and healthy eating has opened at Opéra. Children can read books on bikes and colour in giant pictures that well help them to find their way around the city. On the menu are healthy and seasonal products, mostly organic, cooked up by EXKi. Fresh fruit tarts, chocolate cake, tarte tatin, cheesecake, *merveilleux*, lemon meringue pie, muffins… their mouth-watering desserts appeal to both kids and parents.

22, Rue de la Chaussée-d'Antin, 9ᵉ.
+33 1 44 83 09 01.
Open Mon–Fri 8am–9pm, Sat 10am–9pm.
lamaisonvelibexki.paris.fr

Little chefs!

After seeing Ratatouille, do your little ones fancy themselves to be top chefs? Work on this idea to acquaint your kids with French and foreign food. They'll be more appreciative of the dishes you cook for them, and who knows, they may even help you to make them.

LITTLE CHEF AT THE RITZ

After several years of refurbishment works, the Ritz in Place Vendôme is reopening its doors to wealthy guests in 2016. But did you know that your children can have the privilege of entering the Michelin-starred kitchen of this famous hotel? The École Ritz-Escoffier offers kids aged 6–17 the chance to meet the chef and his team and discover the secrets behind their dishes. The young apprentices learn the basics of French *haute cuisine* and take their work home with them for the family to taste. An idea for a memorable learning experience!

15, Place Vendôme, 1ᵉʳ. +33 1 43 16 30 50.
€100 for a 2 1/2-hr workshop.
ritzescoffier.com/fr-FR/ateliers-cours-cuisine/pour-les-enfants

APPRENTICE SUSHI CHEF

Under the supervision of an Asian sushi chef and equipped with aprons and utensils suitable for their age, your children can learn to make genuine 'Japanese' dishes: Philadelphia rolls; salmon, avocado and chip California rolls, and the dreaded Nutella California rolls.

By making simple and delicious dishes, your children will develop their sense of taste and it will be a treat for them to make what they've learned for you at home.

Le Labo Culinaire
11, Avenue Stéphane-Mallarmé, 17ᵉ.
+33 1 46 22 20 94.
€29 per person. laboculinaire.com

COOK AT A PARIS DEPARTMENT STORE

BHV Marais has fitted out a kitchen that allows Parisians young and old to come and learn cooking techniques. Throughout the year, cooking lessons are given different themes, including decorated cupcakes, Halloween pastries, birthday cakes and Christmas dishes.

BHV Marais
52, Rue de Rivoli, 4ᵉ. bhv.fr

125

CUOCHI IN ERBA

Fresh pasta, pizza, gelato, Sicilian cannoli… so many mouth-watering Italian specialities. Wouldn't it be great if your kids made them for you? The **Polimnia** association teaches them the basics of Italian cuisine, and the language. Lessons are given in Italian to children aged 5–11.

20, Square Dunois, 13ᵉ.
+33 6 68 10 08 80.
€24 per person.
polimnia.eu

DUCASSE'S HEIR?

Famous **chef Alain Ducasse** has his own cooking school in the sixteenth arrondissement where children aged 6 and over can take part in courses. They are shown how to prepare a whole range of healthy and delicious snacks and typical dishes to celebrate Christmas, Easter and the Epiphany. The school also offers 'four-handed lessons' for parents and children.

64, Rue du Ranelagh, 16ᵉ.
+33 1 44 90 91 00.
€90–110.
ecolecuisine-alainducasse.com

WE LIKE LENÔTRE

Lenotre also offers cooking and pastry-making courses for children aged 8 and over. Young chocoholics, fruit fans, budding bakers and street food lovers are introduced to the idea of 'healthy eating' while enjoying a friendly learning atmosphere.

Pavillon Élysée, 10, Av. des Champs-Élysées, 8ᵉ.
+33 1 30 81 44 96.
€40–80. ecolelenotre.com

MAKE ME A BOGATO CAKE

In a more relaxed atmosphere than the one found at the grand culinary establishments, **Chez Bogato** holds cooking workshops for children aged 4 and over. Kids' favourite ingredients are used, such as Nutella, Chamallows and Tagada strawberries to make such things as magnificent cupcakes. You can also request a private kitchen for a birthday celebration, where everyone gets a chef's hat.

7, Rue Liancourt, 14ᵉ.
+33 1 40 47 03 51.
Ateliers le mer. €26.
chezbogato.fr

PIZZA WORKSHOPS
PICCOLO DI REBELLATO

Here's a workshop where kids learn to make Neapolitan pizzas, the real ones.
After putting on a hat and apron, the dough is made, ready for a topping: tomatoes, mozzarella di bufala and Sicilian black olives. Only Italian products with protected designation of origin are used. The pizzas are then put into the wood-fired oven before the most important part: tasting. No sweet tooth will be left unsatisfied because Nutella pizza is on the menu. The junior cooks may leave with their hands full of flour, but they won't be empty. Each is given a pizza box full of surprises.

Pizzeria di Rebellato
138, Rue de la Pompe, 16ᵉ.
1-hr workshops, one Sun per month
for children aged 4–10.
Enrol at piccolodirebellatto@gmail.com
pizzeria.rebellato.fr

COOKING LESSONS AT HOME

Cook and Go is a company that lets you hold cooking lessons at your home with your kids. The fully stocked kits they provide contain all the necessary ingredients and tips you need for the lesson.

175, Rue Saint-Charles, 15ᵉ. 69,
Rue Lafayette, 9ᵉ.
17, Bd Saint-Jacques, 14ᵉ. €39.
cook-and-go.com

127

[We show you how]

Easter ideas

*Till April's dead, change not a thread…
but it shouldn't stop you from wanting
to enjoy the first rays of spring sunshine.
Your little chicks' yearnings for nature,
chocolate treats and new outings need
to be satisfied.*

GET CRACKING!

To celebrate the arrival of spring, get the
kids working on making Easter eggs with
a very simple method: by cracking eggs.
The shells can be filled with melted chocolate
and anything else that will fit in their little
hands, such as brown sugar, chopped
hazelnuts, cinnamon and other nuts. You
can also find silicone moulds with cavities
shaped like chicks, baskets and other Easter-
themed objects, or use an ice tray. They're
ready after five hours in the fridge.
The artists will jump at the chance to
decorate eggs with painted or coloured eggs

(using food colouring), which they can lay inside nests made of feathers. The websites **My Little Day** and **My Little Kids** are filled with wonderful ideas: pastel-coloured eggs and eggs with hair made from sprouts, origami rabbits and rabbit ears for Alice in Wonderland's little companions.
mylittleday.fr
mylittlekids.fr/diy-paques

FINGER-LICKING GOOD
Little chocolate lovers can discover the 4,000-year-old story of cocoa at the **Musée du Chocolat**. Inside this former Turkish bath on Boulevard de Bonne-Nouvelle (this isn't made up!) in the tenth arrondissement, they go on a treasure hunt and 'Choco Story' workshops, explaining the history of celebrating with chocolate in all its forms. There are also cooking courses held for budding pastry chefs (see pp 125 and 126) and workshops for two, which allow parents to try their hand too.
Musée du Chocolat
28, Boulevard de Bonne-Nouvelle, 10ᵉ.
+33 1 42 29 68 60.
museeduchocolat.fr

La Pâtisserie des Rêves 111, Rue de Longchamp,16ᵉ. +33 1 47 04 00 24.
lapatisseriedesreves.com

L'Atelier des chefs
Different Paris locations (Saint-Lazare, Printemps Nation and Penthièvre).
atelierdeschefs.fr

L'Atelier des Sens 32, Rue Vignon, 9ᵉ.
+33 1 40 21 08 50
atelier-des-sens.com

BEST OUTINGS
According to French tradition, church bells fly to Rome during Lent and scatter chocolate eggs as they return on Easter Sunday. Kit your hunters out with pretty baskets or with an egg carton they've decorated themselves and send them on their way... Check out websites devoted to family outings for Easter egg hunts organized in public places in Paris and the surrounding area (public gardens, parks, cafés and town halls). But beware;
they can sometimes be disappointing. Consult Internet forums so you can avoid disappointment.
A huge egg hunt is held in the magnificent grounds of the **Château de Vaux-le-Vicomte**, in the Seine-et-Marne region, and egg decorating workshops are held on the Saturday, Sunday and Monday of the Easter long weekend. With the excuse of these chocolate treats (from Léonidas), you can allow your children to discover one of the most beautiful châteaux in the Paris area.

[We show you how]

Secours Populaire Easter egg hunt
on the Champ-de-Mars, École Militaire end, 7ᵉ.
€5 donation.

Mairie (town hall) 7ᵉ arrondissement
Easter Wednesday 2–4pm, egg-painting
workshops every half an hour and Easter egg
hunt at 4pm in the Mairie garden.
116, Rue de Grenelle, 7ᵉ. Registration +33 1 53
58 75 60.

Musée de Montmartre
Easter egg hunt in the Jardins Renoir. 12–14,
Rue Cortot, 18ᵉ.
Registration required :
accueil@montmartre-guide.com

Poule Mouillette
Tea room and shop
Easter workshop and indoor egg hunt 13,
Rue des Récollets, 10ᵉ.
+33 9 83 22 32 17.
Poulemouillette.fr

Château de Vaux-le-Vicomte
77950 Maincy.
+33 1 64 14 41 90.
Open every day 8 Mar–8 Nov,
10am–6pm. vaux-le-vicomte.com

ROCK'N'ROLL CHICKS

Round off an egg hunt by listening to an
orchestra of Chantilly chickens or with a
chicken or rabbit race. We're not joking;
these shows are part of the entertainment
programme at the **Potager des Princes**
animal park in Chantilly, Oise region,
located about 200 metres from the Grands
Écuries. Place bets on the bravest-looking
chicken or the cutest rabbit: your children
will become real bookmakers for a day.
They'll also have great fun visiting the
farmyard and rabbit village. A Japanese
garden, bamboo maze, tropical garden, an
amazing vegetable garden and orchards
complete the tour.

130

In short, this is a delightful place where you can also hire a Gothic Revival-style cottage containing a double and a single bed.
Le Potager des Princes
17, Rue de la Faisanderie, 60500 Chantilly.
+ 33 3 44 57 39 66.
Open late Mar–early Nov.
Every day 10am–12 noon and 2–7pm.
Wed, Sat, Sun and every day during the school holidays, 3 shows at 3pm and 4pm.
potagerdesprinces.com

Chapter 5
Decorating, gifts and new look

Decorating ideas

Doing up a child's room is never easy. You've got so many ideas but need to know good places to go for the perfect furniture, lighting and accessories.

LA DÎNETTE DE SOPHIE
Here you will find the best advice for decorating your kid's room. You can browse among second-hand objects that you can have upcycled to suit your taste. One thing is certain: your room will never look like the latest Ikea catalogue.
41, Rue de la Fontaine-au-Roi, 11ᵉ.
+33 1 55 28 61 78.
Open Mon 1-7.30pm, Tues-Sat 11am-7.30pm.
ladinettedesophie.com

SERENDIPITY
Serendipity is a shop that opened in 2004 in a former parking garage on the Left Bank. It offers a selection of furniture and accessories for decorating a child's room that combine vintage, design and contemporary creations.
81-83, Rue du Cherche-Midi, 6ᵉ.
+33 1 42 22 12 18.
Open Tues-Sat 11am-7pm. serendipity.fr

BALOUGA
The favourite online shopping site for fans of design for children has its own shop and showroom. It displays a selection of furniture and accessories, and offers advice. You can place an order and collect it there without having to pay for delivery.
1, Rue Notre-Dame-de-Nazareth, 3ᵉ. balouga.com

PETIT PAN
Petit Pan's trademark style is based on patterns, colours and prints: spots, circles, crescents, diamonds, flowers and pinstripes are interlaced in a symphony of colours. This shop offers all the most original fabrics to make household linen, curtains for children's rooms, cushion covers, throws, kites...
7, Rue de Prague, 12ᵉ.
10 *bis*, Rue Yvonne-Le-Tac,18ᵉ.
29, Rue François-Miron, 4ᵉ.
Open Tues-Sat 10.30am-7pm. petitpan.com

LAURETTE
Founded in 2004, this furniture company manufactures deluxe pieces for children's rooms that combine contemporary trends with vintage and retro styles. From production to finishings, each piece is lovingly crafted with attention to quality and details.
18, Rue Mabillon, 6ᵉ.
+33 1 46 34 35 22.
Open Tues-Sat 11am-7pm.
laurette-deco.com

Treasure trove

You have Colette and Merci, but little Parisians are also entitled to their own concept store to find the most outrageous items ever designed for them anywhere in the world. These are also good addresses to know if you want to find special birthday or Christmas presents.

BONTON

Bonton is a spin-off of Bonpoint. In fact, it was opened by Thomas is the son of Marie-France and Bernard Cohen, Bonpoint's founders. The essence of the brand is style, expertise and well-cut clothes. And with its main ingredients of colour, exuberance and humour, the Bonton style is a favourite with the stars. Besides keeping up with the latest trends, Bonton collections bring pizzazz to the basics.
84 bis, Rue de Grenelle, 7ᵉ.
5, Boulevard des Filles-du-Calvaire, 3ᵉ.
+33 1 42 72 34 69.
Open Mon–Sat 10am–7pm. bonton.fr

LILLI BULLE

You'll find the shop window at Lilli Bulle, a creative space for kids, absolutely irresistable. You'll find hip toys and designer clothing, everything imaginable for your little ones. You'll also find original accessories you won't see anywhere else, making it the perfect place to purchase that special gift.
3, Rue de la Forge-Royale, 11ᵉ.
+33 1 43 73 71 63.
Open Tues–Fri 10am–1.30pm and 3–7pm, Sat 11.30am–7pm.
lillibulle.com

135

POP MARKET

Located by the Canal Saint-Martin, this concept store has a large designer selection for kids: clothes, toys, accessories, costumes, books and sweets, making it almost impossible to leave empty-handed. You'll also find what you need for DIY sessions with your kids.
50, Rue Bichat, 10ᵉ.
Open Mon–Fri 11–3pm and 4–7.30pm, Sat 11am–7.30pm. / popmarket.fr

PARIS RENDEZ-VOUS

The Hôtel de Ville's concept store offers lots
of ideas for presents that are representative
of Paris: giant wall posters for colouring
in, wooden boats inspired by the ones seen
sailing on the city's ponds, Fermob chairs
(child-sized versions of the ones found in
the city's parks), Teddy bears made in the
Jura regions, children's books from Paris's
museums… a wide selection of French-made
products inspired by the cultural heritage of
Paris to make your kids proud of their city.
Hôtel de Ville, 29, Rue de Rivoli, 4ᵉ.
Open Mon–Sat 10am–7pm. boutique.paris.fr

BIBI

This concept store is entirely devoted to
kids. It isn't big, but it has an ideal selection
for you to find fun gifts for the little ones.
There are lots of completely wacky imported
products and you get to listen to Bibi's
playlist as you shop.
35, Rue de Bretagne, 3ᵉ.
+33 1 42 77 12 82.
Open Mon 1–8pm, Tues–Fri 11–8pm, Sat
10.30am–8pm, Sun 9am–7pm.
bibiparis.fr

NOT SO BIG

The brand that's all the rage in Japan has
a shop in the Montorgueil neighbourhood.
Everything you find here comes in pretty
patterns and beautiful colours – the height of
junior fashion.
38, Rue Tiquetonne, 2ᵉ. +33 1 42 33 34 26.
Open Mon–Sat 11am–7.30pm.
bynotsobig.com

MILLIMÈTRES

Since 2011, this concept store for kids
has been showcasing objects and clothes
designed between the 1950s and the present
day. You'll find all you need to decorate
rooms for children, dress them in the hippest
brands and to send them to school in style.
19, Rue Milton, 9ᵉ. +33 1 71 70 96 99.
Open Mon–Sat 11am–7pm. millimetres.fr

A new look

Does your kid need a haircut and a new wardrobe? Here's a selection of the cutest Paris establishments for the little dears.

HAIR IN STYLE
MUM & BABE
Mum relaxes at the hairdresser while the kids get spruced up. Is that your dream? It's a reality here, because the staff at this salon look after your kids while you take care of your hair and body.
3, Rue Keller, 11ᵉ.
+33 1 43 38 83 55.
€16 for babies, €20 for children.

SIMON, COIFFEUR DE FAMILLE
This hairdressing salon welcomes every generation. This joyful establishment, which was one of the pioneers in the art of cropping kids' hair, is swarming with kids, either under the hairdryer or leafing through magazines, just like mum.
16, Rue Vavin, 6ᵉ.
+33 1 53 10 08 12.
€15 for babies, €27 for children.

BONTON COIFFEUR
At the back of this immense children's store is a hairdressing salon. It's the ideal place to have your child given a new look while you head off to find Bonton's latest dress or cute top.
5, Boulevard des Filles-du-Calvaire, 3ᵉ.
+33 1 42 72 99 79.
€15 for babies, €25 for children.

DRESSING UP
CENTRE COMMERCIAL KIDS
You probably know the Centre Commercial shop very near the Canal Saint-Martin. Well, they've expanded with a second shop devoted to kids. They mainly stock clothes for newborns up to children aged 14, and only made in France or other European countries.
22, rue Yves-Toudic, 10ᵉ.
+33 1 42 06 23 81.
Open Tues–Sat 10.30am–7.30pm, Sun 2–7pm.
centrecommercial.cc

ZEF
Add a touch of fantasy, Italian inspiration and a retro, bohemian air to your kids' wardrobe.
55 *bis*, Rue des Saints-Pères, 6ᵉ.
Zef-surplus: outlet shop
32, Rue de Richelieu, 1ᵉʳ.

MILK ON THE ROCKS NYC
Comfortable fabrics, surprising colours, fun and pop-rock inspiration for this original brand. Your kids will love it.
7, Rue Mézières, 6ᵉ.
milkontherocks.net

Index of featured addresses

IN THE SAME COLLECTION

Paris à l'air libre
Lindsey Tramuta

The best ideas for living in Paris (almost) like living in the country.

AVAILABLE IN ENGLISH
AVAILABLE FOR DOWNLOAD FROM APP STORE

Paris by Bike Vélib'

7 cycling routes to discover a different side to Paris.

My Little Day
Gabriella Toscan du Plantier, Dorothée Monestier, Iris De Moüy

Everything you need to organize your child's birthday party.

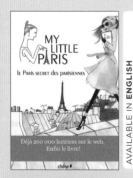

AVAILABLE IN ENGLISH
AVAILABLE FOR DOWNLOAD FROM APP STORE

My Little Paris
My Little Paris, Kanako

The best secret and out-of-the-ordinary addresses in Paris.

AVAILABLE IN ENGLISH
AVAILABLE FOR DOWNLOAD FROM APP STORE

Paris pour les hommes
Thierry Richard, Aseyn, Juliette Ranck

The first city guide especially for men who love Paris.

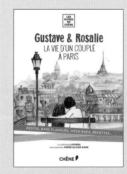

Gustave & Rosalie
Gustave & Rosalie

A practical guide for couples in Paris.

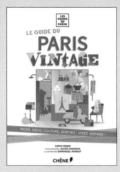

Le Guide du Paris vintage

**Cathy Robin,
Julien Chamoux**

Fashion, decoration, culture,
outings: vive le vintage!

Les Nouveaux Créateurs
à Paris

Régis Pennel, Philippe Zorzetto

50 addresses you really need
to know.

Guide de la Scandinavie
à Paris

**Katia Barillot, Axel Gyldén,
Pierre-Olivier Signe**

The 50 best addresses.

Guide du Japon à Paris

**Minako Norimatsu,
Pierre-Olivier Signe**

The best of Japan in Paris
through 200 addresses.

Guide de l'Italie à Paris

**Valérie Vangreveninge,
Pierre-Olivier Signe**

La *dolce vita* in Paris through
150 addresses.

Guide des USA à Paris

**Noélie Viallet,
Pierre-Olivier Signe**

The best of New York and the USA
in Paris through 200 addresses.

AVAILABLE IN ENGLISH

Le Guide du Paris sucré

**Caroline Mignot,
Pierre-Olivier Signe**

Indulge your sweet tooth in Paris.

AVAILABLE IN ENGLISH

AVAILABLE FOR DOWNLOAD
FROM APP STORE

Paris fait son cinéma

**Barbara Boespflug, Béatrice
Billon, Pierre-Olivier Signe**

101 legendary Parisian addresses that
inspired the great films.

L'Art de rester zen à Paris

**Alexandra de Lassus,
Charlotte du Jour**

All the advice you need to keep
a Zen attitude.

Acknowledgements

The publishers would like to thank the Mairie de Paris and the whole team at Velib' & moi for their responsiveness and energy, and Marie Simon for her help in editing.

The Brand Marketing and Communication Department of the Mairie de Paris would like to thank JCDecaux for their assistance.

English translation and proofreading:
John Ripoll and Laura Gladwin for Cillero & de Motta

Éditions du Chêne
CEO: Fabienne Kriegel
Editorial Manager: Nathalie Lefebvre
Editing and additional writing: Aude Le Pichon
Editorial Assistant: Françoise Mathay, assisted by Aurélie Le Marchand
Art Direction: Claire Mieyeville and Sabine Houplain
Graphic design: Mozilla
Proofreading: Blandine Houdart
Production: Éric Peyronnet
Photoengraving: Quat'coul

Mairie de Paris
Information and Communication Director: Jean-Marie Vernat
Managing Editor: Gildas Robert, Brand Marketing and Communication Manager
Project Manager: Wilfried Hubert, Project Manager and Editorial and Design
Assistant and Licensing Agent for the book: Élisabeth Dubost, Licensing Agent for P'tit Vélib' – Arboresens
Illustrations: Aurélie Castex and Claire Laude – Mesdemoiselles – mesdemoiselles.fr
Cartographie: JCDecaux